STOP OVERTHINKING YOUR LIFE

11 PRACTICAL STEPS TO OVERCOME ANXIETY, MAKE CONFIDENT DECISIONS, STOP SPIRALING OUT OF CONTROL, AND FINALLY GET A GOOD NIGHT'S SLEEP

CAMRYN KELLEY

CONTENTS

INTRODUCTION

It was a typical Monday morning and I was rushing to get out the door, grabbing my coffee and checking my phone for the hundredth time. I was already feeling overwhelmed before my day had even begun, and I knew it was going to be a long and stressful week. As I stepped outside, I was hit with a realization that was both alarming and all too familiar - I couldn't remember the last time I had felt truly relaxed. I was stuck in a cycle of constant stress and anxiety, and I couldn't see a way out.

Sound familiar? If you're nodding your head right now, then we have something in common. Mental health is a serious topic, but let's be honest—it can also be a real pain in the brain. Anxiety and stress are like pesky little houseguests that won't leave, and they can make life feel like a never-ending game of Whack-A-Mole. But don't worry, I've got you covered. This book is like a Swiss Army Knife for your mental health, packed with all the tips and tricks you need to win the battle against anxiety and stress.

Overthinking is like a game of Jenga, but instead of wooden blocks, you're pulling out hair. Chronic stress can make you feel like you're stuck in a never-ending cycle of, "Oh no, what now?" It can leave you feeling burnt out, exhausted, and ready to move to a deserted island.

It's easy to feel like you're the only one constantly trapped in your thoughts, but recent studies show this is far from the truth. In fact, imagine walking into a room of one hundred 25-35-year-olds. At least 73 of them struggle with overthinking. And if we're talking about 45-55-year-olds, at least 52 are also chronic overthinkers. It's not just a handful of people, it's the majority. Overthinking is a pandemic that's taking over our minds and ruining our lives, one thought at a time.

Have you ever found yourself in a situation where you just can't seem to make a decision? You're stuck in this never-ending cycle of overthinking and rethinking every possible outcome and scenario. Before you know it, hours have passed and you're still no closer to making a choice. This is what we call analysis paralysis, and it's a result of overthinking.

But let's take a step back. Why do we overthink in the first place? It's often because we're afraid of making the wrong decision and facing the consequences that come with it. Our brains are wired to protect us from danger, so it's no surprise that we're prone to overthinking when we feel threatened. However, the constant state of fear that comes with overthinking can have a significant impact on our mental health, relationships, and overall well-being. Think about it, when you're consumed with worry and anxiety, it's hard to focus on anything else. You might find yourself struggling to connect with others and be present in the moment. The constant chatter in your head makes it hard to think clearly, leaving you feeling tired, overwhelmed, and unable to solve problems effectively.

But fear not! This book is here to help you turn the tide. I've brought together the latest research and expert insights to help you understand these issues and learn how to manage them. I'll cover everything from the basics of anxiety and stress to the latest treatments and therapies. And most importantly, I'll talk about what you can do right now to take control of your own mental health and lead a happier, more fulfilling life.

By the time you finish this book, you'll have a toolkit full of techniques and strategies that you can use to manage your anxiety and stress. You'll learn how to identify the root cause of your anxiety, and how to develop a personalized plan for managing it. You'll discover the power of mindfulness, self-care, and exercise in reducing stress, and you'll learn how to prioritize relaxation and fun in your daily life. Most importantly, you'll gain a sense of control and empowerment over your life. You'll learn how to recognize the warning signs of stress and anxiety, and how to intervene before they spiral out of control. You'll discover the importance of self-compassion, and how to be kinder and more patient with yourself.

So grab a cup of tea (or your preferred stress-relieving beverage), put on your comfiest pajamas, and get ready to start loving your life.

STEP 1

UNDERSTAND IT

> *"I think and think and think, I've thought myself out of happiness one million times, but never once into it."*
>
> — JONATHAN SAFRAN FOER

W e can all relate to this feeling of being stuck in our thoughts and unable to find a way out.Overthinking is a common experience for many of us, and it can often lead to feelings of anxiety, worry, and stress. It's when we find ourselves dwelling or worrying about the same thought repeatedly, and it can be a symptom of depression or anxiety.

There are two types of overthinking: rumination, which involves rehashing past events, and worrying, which is hyper-focusing on an anxious concern about the future. Although thinking, when done right, with logic, awareness, and true open-minded curiosity, can be helpful, overthinking can interfere with us living happy and fulfilling lives. In this chapter, we will explore how much thinking is too much and why it's essential to recognize when we've crossed the line between useful thought and overthinking.

WHAT IS OVERTHINKING?

We all know the feeling, don't we? It's when you just can't seem to stop thinking about something. You ruminate on the same thought repeatedly, like a hamster running on a wheel. It's like your brain is stuck in an endless loop, and you just can't escape.

According to the Cleveland Clinic, overthinking is "to put too much time into thinking about or analyzing something in a way that is more harmful than helpful." It can be a symptom of depression or anxiety and can lead to even more depression and anxiety. So, it's not just a harmless habit; it can have serious consequences.

WHY DO WE OVERTHINK?

Do you ever find yourself overthinking things? Wondering why your mind won't stop spinning, even when you know it's not helping? Let's take a closer look at *why* we overthink.

First up, childhood trauma. Many people who have a severe habit of overthinking developed the habit early in life, often as a child. And they usually developed it because, at the time, it was the only way they had to deal with scary, difficult experiences. So they kept overthinking as a way to feel like they are dealing with stress or anxiety, and it became a hardwired habit.

But childhood trauma isn't the only culprit. Ongoing stress as an adult can also lead to overthinking. Sometimes, we get so caught up in our stress that we become obsessed with it. We think about the problem so much that it becomes all-consuming, and we can't think about anything else.

And then there's the illusion of control. Overthinking gives us the illusion that we have control over a situation and keeps our feelings of helplessness at bay. We believe that if we just think long and hard enough, we can find a solution to the problem. But often, this just keeps us stuck in problem-solving mode rather than action-taking mode and we never end up actually doing anything to solve the problem.

Perfectionists also end up overthinking as a way to distract from having to feel less than perfect about their work. They keep working on the problem, hoping to avoid potential failure, but the reality is that they're delaying the inevitable.

Excessive fear of conflict leads to a lot of unnecessary thinking about how to avoid it. People with this fear tend to overthink the potential scenarios and outcomes of a conflict, trying to come up with the "perfect" solution that avoids conflict entirely.

Finally, some people get stuck in the habit of overthinking because it has secondary or non-obvious benefits. For example, it can lead to sympathy and pity from other people in their lives, which feels good. Or it can be an excuse for procrastinating or avoiding decisions.

So, there you have it. There are many reasons why we over-think, but it's important to understand why we do it in order to stop the habit.

HOW MUCH THINKING IS TOO MUCH?

We all know that thinking is good for us. After all, it's what sets us apart from animals. But when does it cross the line into overthinking territory? This is a complicated question. It's not like a game of Jenga where you can only pull out so many blocks before the whole thing comes tumbling down. It's more like a delicate dance that we have to do with ourselves, and it's a dance that never ends.

So how do we know when we're doing too much of it? Well, the truth is, it's different for everyone. It's not like you can set a timer and say, "Okay, that's enough thinking for today." But there are signs that you can look out for, like feeling mentally exhausted, fixating on things outside of your control, or worrying that jumps from one topic to the next. If any of these sound familiar, then you might be guilty of overthinking.

THE NEUROSCIENCE OF OVERTHINKING

So, we know that overthinking can be a real pain in the brain, but what's actually going on up there? Let's take a look at the neuroscience of overthinking.

First off, it's important to understand that the brain is divided into three major regions: the neocortex, the limbic system, and the brainstem. The neocortex is responsible for higher brain functions like reasoning, decision-making, and problem-solving. The limbic system is where emotions, memories, and habits are formed. The brainstem controls basic life functions like breathing and heart rate.

When we overthink, the prefrontal cortex, the front part of the neocortex, becomes overactive. This is the part of the brain responsible for conscious thought and decision-making. As a result, we become hyper-focused on our thoughts and can't seem to break out of the cycle.

Research has shown that negative thoughts and emotions activate the amygdala, a part of the limbic system which sends a signal to the hypothalamus, which in turn activates the sympathetic nervous system, triggering the body's fight-or-flight response. This is why overthinking can lead to physical symptoms like increased heart rate, sweating, and muscle tension.

The good news is that the brain is plastic, which means it can be rewired. By practicing mindfulness and meditation, you can strengthen the connections between the prefrontal cortex and the amygdala, making it easier to regulate your emotions and break out of the cycle of overthinking.

So, the next time you find yourself lost in a sea of thoughts, take a deep breath and remind yourself that you have the power to retrain your brain.

MAIN SIGNS OF OVERTHINKING

When you are overthinking, there are several signs that indicate you are be doing so. These signs include:

1. You can't seem to think about anything else. Even when you try to focus on other things, your mind drifts back to the same thoughts, and you can't seem to let them go.
2. You find it difficult to relax. You might have trouble sleeping or even find yourself feeling anxious and tense when you're trying to unwind.
3. You feel constantly worried or anxious. Even when there isn't an obvious reason for concern, your mind seems to jump to the worst-case scenario.
4. You fixate on things outside of your control. You might obsess over things that have already happened or things that might happen in the future but that you have no power to change.
5. You feel mentally exhausted. The constant barrage of thoughts and worries can leave you feeling drained and overwhelmed.
6. You have a lot of negative thoughts. You might find yourself focusing on the bad things that could happen rather than the good things already happening around you.
7. You replay situations or experiences in your mind. You might go over past conversations or events, trying to analyze what happened or what you could have done differently.
8. Your worries jump from one topic to the next. You might find that once you've solved one problem, your mind immediately jumps to the next one, without giving you a chance to catch your breath.

9. You think of the worst-case scenario by default. Instead of assuming the best, you automatically assume the worst.

10. You struggle to make decisions, and often second-guess yourself. Even simple decisions can feel overwhelming, and once you make a decision, you doubt yourself and wonder if you made the right choice.

11. You have trouble concentrating. With so many thoughts swirling around in your head, it can be difficult to focus on any one thing.

12. You feel on edge, irritable, and easily emotionally triggered. The stress and tension of overthinking can leave you feeling short-tempered and easily upset.

13. You seek repeated reassurance from others. You might find yourself constantly asking for advice or reassurance from others, rather than trusting your own judgment.

STORY TIME

Reading about other people's experiences can be a powerful way to help us understand our own struggles. When it comes to overthinking, hearing about other people who have been through it can make us feel less alone, less crazy, and more hopeful. In this section, we'll look at three stories of over-thinkers, each with their own unique reasons for overthinking and their own way of dealing with it. These stories are not only interesting but can also offer insights into how we can better manage our own overthinking.

Alicia was a high achiever from a young age, always working to get perfect grades and do everything right. This perfectionism continued into her adult life, causing her to overthink everything she did, from sending emails to completing projects at work. She felt like she needed to have complete control over everything, and that meant second-guessing herself and others constantly. Alicia felt anxious and stressed all the time, and her overthinking made her feel like she was never good enough.

David grew up in a chaotic home with parents who fought constantly. He developed a habit of overthinking as a way to control the situations around him, feeling like if he could just think about things enough, he could prevent any more chaos from happening. As an adult, he continued to overthink every aspect of his life, from his relationships to his work. David felt like he was always on edge, waiting for something bad to happen, and his overthinking only made this feeling worse.

Nina had experienced trauma in her past, causing her to constantly ruminate on the negative events that had happened to her. She couldn't stop replaying the same scenarios in her head, wondering what she could have done differently. Nina felt like she couldn't escape her own mind, constantly reliving her traumas and feeling like she was stuck in the past.

Despite their different reasons for overthinking, all three of them found ways to manage their habits. Alicia started therapy to learn to let go of her need for control and to be kinder to herself. David started practicing mindfulness and meditation to learn to be present in the moment and not get caught up in his anxious thoughts. Nina found support in a trauma-focused therapy group, where she learned coping mechanisms to help her break out of her negative thought patterns.

The stories we've looked at in this section show us that over-thinking can take many forms and have many different causes. However, they also demonstrate that it's possible to break free from the cycle of obsessive thinking and find healthier ways of managing our thoughts. Whether it's by seeking therapy, practicing mindfulness, or simply finding ways to distract ourselves, there are many strategies we can use to quiet our minds and live more peaceful lives. By sharing our stories and supporting one another, we can create a community that helps us all find the peace of mind we deserve.

Final thoughts

By now, you have a clear understanding of overthinking, what causes it, and how it may be affecting your life. Remember, it's important to find a balance between useful thought and over-thinking. When useful thought goes too far, it turns into over-thinking. And overthinking can lead to anxiety, depression, and can impact your physical health as well.

If you feel like you're already experiencing some of the signs of overthinking, don't worry. You're not alone. Overthinking is a habit that can be unlearned with practice and self-awareness.

As we move into the next chapter, you'll be able to understand the different triggers and patterns that cause your overthink-ing. I'll provide you with actionable steps to start working with them so that you can move towards a happier and more fulfilling life.

But for now, take a deep breath, and remind yourself that you have the power to change. Start small and take the first step. You've got this!

STEP 2

GET TO YOUR CORE

The way we think about our lives shapes our perceptions and determines how we experience the world. The previous chapter discussed the basics of overthinking and how it affects us. This chapter will delve deeper into recognizing the warning signs and understanding the causes of overthinking. We'll discuss the triggers of overthinking and how our beliefs shape the way we think, the emotions we feel, and the actions we take.

With the help of the right techniques, you can examine and manage your thoughts more effectively. So, let's get started and understand our story to take a step toward overcoming overthinking.

WHAT OVERTHINKING IS DOING TO YOU AND YOUR LIFE

As we saw in the previous chapter, overthinking is more than just a minor inconvenience. It can have a significant impact on your mental and physical well-being. While it may seem like just an excessive amount of thinking, the reality is that over-thinking can wreak havoc on your life.

Overthinking can affect every aspect of your life, from your sleep quality to your relationships. Here are some of the effects that chronic overthinking can have on your mental and physical health:

- **Stress and anxiety:** Overthinking can lead to feelings of stress and anxiety, which can lead to physical symptoms such as a racing heart, sweating, and muscle tension. This can, in turn, lead to an increased risk of heart disease, high blood pressure, and headaches.
- **Depression:** Chronic overthinking can lead to feelings of hopelessness and worthlessness, which can contribute to the development of depression.
- **Insomnia:** Overthinking can make it difficult to fall asleep or stay asleep, which can contribute to insomnia.
- **Digestive problems:** Overthinking can lead to digestive problems such as irritable bowel syndrome, acid reflux, and other gastrointestinal disorders.

- **Reduced productivity:** When you're constantly overthinking, it's difficult to focus on the task at hand. This can lead to a decrease in productivity and performance at work or school.

Now we know that overthinking can have serious effects on both our mental and physical health. However, because these effects can be subtle and difficult to recognize, it's essential to take a closer look at the specific areas of our lives that are being impacted.

A personal quiz

To help you identify the effects of overthinking on your life, I've created a quiz for you to rate yourself in various categories. Take a moment to honestly assess how you're doing in each area and rate yourself as mild, moderate, or severe. Remember, this is not a diagnosis but rather a tool to help you understand how overthinking may be impacting your life.

	Mild	Moderate	Severe
Lack of focus			
Irritability			
Stress			
Anxiety			
Insomnia			
Undereating			
Overeating			
Racing thoughts			
Digestive issues			
Hyperactivity			
Indecision			
Procrastination			
Analysis paralysis			
Brain fog			
High blood pressure/ chest pain			
Skin disorders - eczema, psoriasis, etc.			
Increased heart rate			
Dizziness			
Headaches			
Nausea			
Fatigue			
Depression			

Once you've rated yourself on each category, take a step back and look at the results. Are there any areas in which you rated yourself as severe? These may be areas in which overthinking is having a particularly strong impact on your life.

Remember, this checklist is not meant to be a substitute for professional help. If you find that you are struggling with any of the items on the checklist, it may be helpful to talk to a mental health professional to help you develop a plan for addressing these issues.

UNDERSTAND YOUR CORE BELIEFS ABOUT LIFE

In order to truly understand your story and overcome over-thinking, it is important to take a deeper look at your core beliefs. Core beliefs are the deeply held, fundamental beliefs about ourselves, others, and the world around us. These beliefs are often formed early in life and can be heavily influenced by our experiences and interactions with the world.

Some common examples of core beliefs include "I am not good enough", "I am unlovable", "The world is a dangerous place", "I have to be perfect to be accepted", and "I am helpless". These beliefs can be deeply ingrained and impact every aspect of our lives, from our relationships to our careers and beyond.

It's important to recognize that these core beliefs are not neces-sarily objective truths but rather our own personal interpreta-tions of the world around us. They can be limiting and hold us back, preventing us from living our lives to the fullest.

By identifying and examining our core beliefs, we can begin to challenge and shift them in more positive and empowering ways. This can open up new possibilities and help us move past the overthinking and self-doubt that may be holding us back.

Reframing and shifting unhelpful core beliefs

It's important to understand that your core beliefs about yourself and the world can be changed. Cognitive Behavioral Therapy (CBT) is a form of therapy that can help you reframe and shift unhelpful core beliefs.

CBT core belief exercises can help you change the negative self-talk and negative thought patterns that contribute to over-thinking. Here are some CBT core belief exercises that you can try:

Thought Record: Start by identifying a negative thought that you have about yourself or a situation. Write it down. Then, ask yourself the following questions:

- What evidence do I have that supports this thought?
- What evidence do I have that contradicts this thought?
- What would I say to a friend who had this thought?
- What is a more balanced and realistic thought that I can replace this negative thought with?

Behavioral Experiments: A behavioral experiment is a way to test your negative beliefs by putting them to the test in real-life situations.

For example, if you have a core belief that you're not good enough, you might try a behavioral experiment where you sign up for a new activity or hobby that you've been wanting to try. By doing this, you're challenging your negative belief and giving yourself the opportunity to prove to yourself that you're capable and deserving.

Remember, reframing and shifting unhelpful core beliefs is a process, and it takes time. Be patient and compassionate with yourself as you work on changing your thought patterns.

REIMAGINING YOUR CORE BELIEFS: A HANDS-ON EXERCISE

Welcome to the interactive portion of this chapter! This section is designed to help you put into practice the knowledge you have gained so far about understanding your story and shifting unhelpful core beliefs.

We will be focusing on two CBT (Cognitive Behavioral Therapy) core belief exercises. These exercises are meant to help you reframe your negative thoughts and replace them with more positive ones.

Exercise 1: Evidence For and Against

In this exercise, you will begin by writing down a negative thought you have about yourself or a situation and then listing evidence for and against that thought. For example, if your negative thought is "I am not good enough," you can write down evidence for that thought, such as "I have failed in the past," and evidence against that thought, such as "I have achieved many things in my life."

To rework this exercise to suit your needs, try to come up with your own negative thoughts and evidence for and against those thoughts. The key is to be honest with yourself and look for evidence that supports and contradicts your negative thoughts.

Exercise 2: Positive Affirmations

This exercise involves creating positive statements about yourself and repeating them to yourself regularly. For example, you can create positive affirmations such as "I am capable," "I am loved," or "I am worthy."

To rework this exercise to suit your needs, try to create your own positive affirmations. Think about the negative thoughts you have about yourself and create positive statements that contradict those thoughts.

Final thoughts

We have now completed the second step of overcoming overthinking. By understanding your triggers and patterns, you can begin to work with them more effectively. Remember, overthinking is a general label that can be caused by a variety of root causes, so take the time to identify what might be fueling your overthinking.

Don't forget to use the checklist I provided to rate yourself on the different areas that are affected by overthinking. By being aware of the effects of overthinking, you can begin to take steps toward managing it.

Understanding your core beliefs and how they impact your life is also essential in managing overthinking. By recognizing and reframing unhelpful core beliefs, you can begin to shift your thought patterns and overcome overthinking.

As we move forward, our next step is to learn how to examine and manage our thoughts. Join me as I explore the world of thought management in the next chapter.

Remember, taking the first step is always the hardest, but you've already come so far. Keep going, and I'll see you in the next chapter!

STEP 3

IT'S ALL IN YOUR MIND

"Worrying is like a rocking chair. It gives you something to do, but it doesn't get you anywhere," said Van Wilder. And he wasn't wrong. Our thoughts have a tremendous impact on our lives, and the way we think shapes our perception of reality.

In this chapter, we'll explore how to work with our thoughts to improve our well-being and achieve our goals. We'll examine the nature of our thoughts, the cognitive biases that can distort them, and the negative inner critic that can sabotage our efforts.

By understanding our thoughts, we can improve our focus, increase our productivity, and lead happier, more fulfilling lives. So let's dive in and learn how to work with our thoughts.

YOUR THOUGHTS DETERMINE YOUR REALITY

Your thoughts are the inner conversations you have with yourself throughout the day. They can be triggered by anything from the events happening around you to the emotions you are feeling. They are the result of your life experiences, what you have been taught, told, learned, and decided about all of this.

It is no secret that your thoughts affect your emotions, but did you know that they can also impact your physical state, choices, and actions? If your thoughts are negative or unhelpful, then that means your actions will be misguided. Research has shown that people who focus on positive thoughts and emotions can improve their physical health, increase productivity, and lead a happier life.

For instance, let's say you're in the middle of an important project, and a thought pops up that you're not good enough to finish it. You start feeling anxious and overwhelmed, and as a result, your productivity goes down. This is because your thoughts have a direct impact on your emotions and behavior.

According to studies, your thoughts can also affect your physical health. Negative thoughts can cause stress, which can, in turn, cause a host of health problems, including high blood pressure, heart disease, and depression.

FAULTY COGNITIVE BIASES

Our brains process an overwhelming amount of information daily, and to do this efficiently, our minds use mental shortcuts or "heuristics."

While these shortcuts are meant to help us make decisions quickly, they can lead to errors in our thinking. These errors are called cognitive biases and can have a significant impact on our decision making, judgment, and beliefs.

Cognitive biases affect the way we perceive information, leading us to make irrational decisions or judgments. They can impact all areas of our lives, from how we form our opinions to how we interact with others.

Here a few common types of cognitive distortions:

- **Confirmation Bias:** This occurs when we actively seek out information that confirms our existing beliefs and ignore or dismiss information that contradicts them.
- **The Halo Effect:** This occurs when we form an overall positive or negative impression of a person, brand, or product based on one trait or characteristic.
- **The Sunk Cost Fallacy:** This occurs when we continue to invest time, money, or resources into a decision that is no longer viable simply because we have already invested in it.
- **Negativity Bias:** This occurs when we focus more on negative information than positive information, even if the positive information is more important or relevant.

- **Hindsight Bias:** This occurs when we believe that we "knew it all along" after an event has occurred, even if we didn't actually predict it beforehand.
- **Availability Bias:** This occurs when we rely on information that is readily available to us, even if it's not the most accurate or representative.
- **Anchoring Bias:** This occurs when we rely too heavily on the first piece of information we receive, even if it's not relevant or accurate.

Cognitive biases can also contribute to the use of logical fallacies. You might have heard of the phrase logical fallacy. But what exactly is it, you might ask.

Logical fallacies are errors in reasoning that can make arguments invalid or unsound. They are often used to manipulate or persuade others, even if the argument being presented is flawed. Understanding logical fallacies is important because it helps us identify and avoid arguments that are misleading or faulty.

Logical fallacies can take many different forms, but they all involve some type of error in reasoning. Some common examples include:

- **Ad Hominem:** Attacking the person making the argument instead of addressing the argument itself.
- **Appeal to Authority:** Relying on the opinion of an authority figure instead of evaluating the argument itself.

- **False Dilemma:** Presenting only two options when other options are available.
- **Slippery Slope:** Suggesting that a minor action will lead to a chain reaction of increasingly negative consequences.
- **Straw Man:** Misrepresenting an opponent's argument to attack a weaker version of it.

HOW TO FACT-CHECK PROPERLY

In today's age of information overload, it's crucial to be able to distinguish accurate information from misinformation. Fact-checking is an essential skill that can help us avoid falling prey to cognitive biases. Here are some strategies to help fact-check information:

1. Use trusted sources: Look for information from reputable sources, such as peer-reviewed journals, academic articles, and trustworthy news outlets. Avoid sources that have a track record of spreading misinformation or conspiracy theories.
2. Verify information with multiple sources: Check the information with multiple sources to ensure that it's accurate and reliable. This can help you detect inconsistencies and falsehoods that might otherwise go unnoticed.
3. Check the source: Look into the source of the information to determine if it's reliable and unbiased. For instance, a study funded by a particular industry may have a bias that affects the results.

Strategies to combat cognitive biases

Becoming aware of our cognitive biases is the first step in combating them. Here are some strategies that can help us combat cognitive biases:

1. Recognize biases in our thinking: We can identify our cognitive biases by examining our thought processes and paying attention to our reactions to different situations.
2. Seek out information that contradicts our existing beliefs: It's important to challenge our assumptions and seek out information that challenges our existing beliefs. This can help us avoid confirmation bias, which occurs when we seek out information that confirms our existing beliefs and ignore information that contradicts them.
3. Fact-check and verify information: As discussed above, fact-checking is essential to avoid misinformation and cognitive biases.
4. Seek out diverse perspectives and opinions: Expose yourself to diverse perspectives and opinions to gain a more complete understanding of an issue. This can help you avoid the halo effect.
5. Ask questions and challenge assumptions: Don't be afraid to ask "Is that really true?" This can help you avoid the sunk cost fallacy, so that you won't continue to invest your resources into a decision that is no longer viable, simply because you have already invested in it.

EXAMINING THE QUALITY OF YOUR THOUGHTS

Our thoughts are powerful and have a significant impact on our emotions, behaviors, and overall well-being. It's important to be aware of the quality of our thoughts and to actively work to improve them.

The negative inner critic is a part of ourselves that often speaks to us in a harsh, critical voice. It can be a powerful force that holds us back from pursuing our goals, causes us to doubt ourselves and our abilities, and undermines our self-esteem. The negative inner critic is often based on negative beliefs we have about ourselves, which can be the result of past experiences, trauma, or other factors. Learning to recognize and manage the negative inner critic is a key part of improving the quality of our thoughts.

The first step in examining the quality of our thoughts is to simply observe them. This means paying attention to the thoughts that come into your mind without judging or reacting to them. When you observe your thoughts, you can start to see patterns and tendencies in your thinking. This can help you to identify unhelpful patterns of thought and to start shifting them.

Once you start observing your thoughts, you can begin to identify which ones are helpful and which ones are harmful. Helpful thoughts are those that support your well-being and help you to achieve your goals. Harmful thoughts, on the other hand, are those that hold you back or cause you to feel anxious, stressed, or depressed. By identifying harmful thoughts, you can start to challenge them and replace them with more helpful ones.

Shifting unhelpful thoughts takes practice and patience, but it can be done with time and effort. One approach is to challenge the thoughts by asking yourself if they are really true or if there is evidence to support them. You can also try to reframe the thoughts in a more positive or constructive way.

For example, if you find yourself thinking "I can't do this," you might try reframing it as "I haven't done this before, but I'm willing to try." Another approach is to focus on the present moment and what you can do in this moment to improve your situation rather than dwelling on negative thoughts about the past or future.

Mastering your focus

The ability to concentrate and direct one's focus is an essential skill for mastering your thoughts. Your thoughts can quickly spiral out of control if you're not able to direct your attention to the things that matter. By focusing on the present moment and becoming more aware of your thoughts, you can learn to steer them in more productive directions. This can help you avoid distractions, negative thinking, and unhelpful thought patterns.

Improving your focus and concentration skills can be a powerful tool in mastering your thoughts.

Here are some strategies you can use to improve your focus and concentration:

1. **Practice mindfulness:** Mindfulness is the practice of being present in the moment and aware of your thoughts and surroundings. By learning to focus on the present moment, you can become more aware of your thoughts and better able to direct them.

2. **Break tasks into smaller steps:** It's much easier to stay focused on a task when you break it down into smaller, more manageable steps. By focusing on one step at a time, you can avoid feeling overwhelmed and stay on task.

3. **Avoid multitasking:** Trying to do multiple things at once can be a recipe for distraction and poor performance. Instead, focus on one task at a time and give it your full attention.

4. **Take breaks:** Taking regular breaks can help you stay focused and avoid burnout. Taking short breaks every hour or so can help you recharge and refocus.

5. **Manage distractions:** Identify the things that distract you and take steps to minimize them. This might mean turning off your phone or closing your email while you're working on an important task.

By implementing these strategies, you can improve your focus and concentration skills and master your thoughts.

MINDFUL MUSINGS: A THOUGHT-TRACKING EXPERIMENT

In this section, I'm going to give you an interactive exercise to put your new knowledge to the test. By tracking your thoughts and reactions, you can start to become more aware of your cognitive biases and how they affect your behavior.

The thought explorer challenge

For the next week, keep a thought journal. Find a notebook or use a note-taking app on your phone where you can record your thoughts. Each day, set aside a few minutes to reflect on your day and write down a few thoughts that came up for you. It can be helpful to note what time of day it was, where you were, and what you were doing when the thought occurred. This will help you start to identify patterns and triggers for your thoughts.

As you record your thoughts, pay attention to the emotions that come up for you as well. Did you feel anxious, sad, or angry? Did you feel happy, excited, or inspired? Note down the emotions you experienced alongside each thought. This will help you become more aware of how your thoughts affect your emotions.

In addition to recording your thoughts and emotions, you can also note any physical reactions you had in response to your thoughts. Did you feel tense or relaxed? Did your heart rate increase or decrease? Did you experience any physical sensations in your body, such as tightness in your chest or butterflies in your stomach? Recording these physical reactions can help you become more aware of the mind-body connection and how your thoughts can impact your physical state.

At the end of the week, take some time to review your thought journal and look for patterns or themes that emerged. To make this exercise more interactive, try creating a chart or table where you can track your thoughts, emotions, and actions over time. You can also try color-coding your thoughts and reactions to help you identify patterns more easily.

Did you notice any recurring thoughts or emotions? Were there any particular times of day or situations that seemed to trigger certain thoughts or emotions? This information can help you identify areas where you may want to focus your efforts on shifting unhelpful thoughts and improving the quality of your thinking. Did you find yourself often feeling happy, sad, anxious, or angry? Did certain emotions trigger any physical sensations, such as a racing heart, tight chest, or tense muscles?

It can also be helpful to note down any practical reactions you had as a result of the thought. Did you take any action, or did you avoid taking action? Did the thought inspire you to seek out more information or to change your behavior in some way?

Remember, the goal of this exercise is not to judge or criticize your thoughts but to become more aware of them and how they impact you. By bringing more conscious awareness to your thoughts and emotions, you can begin to develop a more intentional and positive relationship with your mind. As you become more aware of your thought patterns and reactions, you may start to notice areas where you could use some improvement.

For example, you might notice that you have a tendency to catastrophize or jump to negative conclusions, which can lead to anxiety and avoidance behaviors. By becoming aware of these patterns, you can start to work on shifting your thoughts to be more positive and productive.

So go ahead and start tracking your thoughts and reactions today. With a little bit of effort and self-reflection, you can start to develop a more positive and productive mindset that will serve you well in all areas of your life.

Final thoughts

Learning to work with your thoughts is an essential step on the journey of overcoming overthinking. By taking the time to understand and examine your cognitive biases, track your thoughts and reactions, and identify thoughts, feelings, and situations where you can work to change how you think, you are taking a powerful step towards a more intentional and fulfilling life.

Working with your thoughts is not an easy process, but it's a worthwhile one. By learning to shift unhelpful thoughts and beliefs, you can start to live a life that is more aligned with your values and goals.

Remember that this is an ongoing process, and it's okay to make mistakes along the way. By becoming more aware of your thoughts and emotions, you are taking an important step towards self-discovery and personal growth.

In the next chapter, I'll be exploring the important topic of regulating your emotions. I'll discuss how to identify and work with your emotions in a healthy and constructive way so that you can live a more balanced and fulfilling life.

So take a deep breath, and get ready for the next chapter. The journey is just beginning, and the possibilities are endless.

STEP 4

EMOTIONAL MASTERY

Overthinking is a common human experience, especially in today's fast-paced world, where we are constantly bombarded with information and distractions. We often get lost in our thoughts, worrying about the future, ruminating on the past, and missing out on the present. But in the midst of all this overthinking, we may be missing out on the very things that make life worth living.

As Nitya Prakash once said, "While you were overthinking, you missed everything worth feeling." This quote is a poignant reminder of the importance of being present in the moment and embracing our emotions rather than getting lost in our thoughts.

In this chapter, we will explore the connection between our thoughts and emotions and how to break the cycle of over-thinking. By becoming more mindful of our thoughts and emotions, we can learn to regulate our emotions more effectively and live a more fulfilling life.

WHAT ARE EMOTIONS?

Emotions are a central aspect of our daily lives, influencing the way we perceive the world around us and interact with others. While emotions can be difficult to define, I think Verywell Mind does a good job. According to them, emotions are "a complex psychological state that involves three distinct components: a subjective experience, a physiological response, and a behavioral or expressive response." This means that emotions involve both our thoughts and feelings, as well as physical changes in our bodies and behaviors that reflect how we are feeling.

One of the main functions of emotions is to provide us with information about our internal state and the world around us. For example, if we feel fear or anxiety, this may signal that we are in danger and need to take action to protect ourselves. Alternatively, if we feel happiness, this may signal that our needs are being met and we are safe and secure.

Emotions can also serve a social function, helping us to communicate our thoughts and feelings to others and connect with them on a deeper level. For example, we may use facial expressions, tone of voice, and body language to convey our emotions to others and elicit a response from them and foster human connection.

However, it's important to note that emotions can also have a significant impact on our well-being. Unresolved or chronic emotional states, such as chronic stress or anxiety, can lead to negative physical and psychological health outcomes, including cardiovascular disease, depression, and anxiety disorders.

UNDERSTANDING EMOTIONAL REGULATION

Emotions are not just random feelings that pop up out of nowhere. They are closely tied to our thoughts and beliefs. By curating our thoughts, we can learn to regulate our emotions more effectively. You can start by identifying some of the negative thought patterns that can trigger negative emotions. Write down a few of your negative thoughts that you've noticed lately. Then, write down a more positive, realistic thought that you can replace it with.

Practicing mindfulness can help us control our focus and attention, which is essential for emotional regulation. Try this mindfulness exercise:

Take a deep breath and focus on the sensation of the air moving in and out of your body. Notice any thoughts that arise, but don't engage with them. Just let them pass like clouds in the sky. Do this for a few minutes and notice how you feel afterward.

By practicing mindfulness you are already well on your way towards caring for your mental needs. But remember that taking care of yourself mentally goes hand-in-hand with caring for yourself physically. Poor mental health can cause poor physical health. But improving your physical health can give you the clarity and confidence you need to help improve your mental well-being. Taking care of ourselves both physically and mentally is crucial for emotional regulation. Here are some self-care practices you can try:

- **Exercise:** Getting exercise is a powerful mood booster and stress reliever. Even just a short walk or a few minutes of stretching can make a big difference.
- **Eating well:** Our diet can have a significant impact on our mood and energy levels. Make sure you're eating a healthy, balanced diet with plenty of fruits, vegetables, and whole grains.
- **Getting enough sleep:** Lack of sleep can cause irritability, anxiety, and other negative emotions. Make sure you're getting enough sleep each night to help regulate your emotions.
- **Hydration:** Even mild dehydration can affect our mood and cognitive function. Make sure you're drinking plenty of water throughout the day.

Identifying the need behind the emotion

When exploring our emotions, it's helpful to understand what is behind the emotion. What is the need that's causing you to feel a certain way? Maslow's hierarchy of needs is a well-known theory that describes the different levels of human needs. At the base of the pyramid are our physical needs, such as food, water, and shelter. These are our most basic needs. If these needs are not satisfied, nothing else matters. Every ounce of energy is used to first fulfill those most basic needs. But once those needs are met, we move up to the next level, which is safety. The same goes for this level. If our need of safety is not met, we cannot spend any energy on higher need. Everything in our being seeks to find safety however we can until that need is finally met. The same thing happens as we move up each additional level of the pyramid, which goes to love and belonging, the next is esteem, and the succession moves up to self-actualization. Each level is important to living a happy and fulfilled life, but the higher levels cannot even be attempted without first achieving the ones below it.

Looking at needs in that way can help it make more sense why certain situations can trigger intense emotions or mental spirals. If something happens that, for example, makes you feel like your safety is threatened, then all of the sudden your sense of belonging and love is threatened also. When you're in the middle of a difficult situation it can be difficult to recognize the deeper need that is truly at the heart of why you feel a certain way. But don't worry. That's what I'm here to help you with.

Identifying emotional needs can be challenging, but it's an important step in regulating our emotions. Here are a few strategies to help you get started:

1. **Practice self-reflection:** Take some time each day to reflect on your emotions and what may be causing them.
2. **Pay attention to your physical needs:** Sometimes, emotional needs can be linked to physical needs, such as hunger or exhaustion. Take care of your physical needs and see if that helps regulate your emotions.

3. **Notice patterns:** Do certain situations or people consistently trigger certain emotions in you? Identifying patterns can help you better understand your emotional needs.

4. **Seek support:** Sometimes, it can be helpful to talk to someone else about your emotions and get their perspective.

By identifying our emotional needs, we can better understand and regulate our emotions, leading to a happier and healthier life.

PROCESSING AND RELEASING EMOTIONS

We've all had moments where we've felt overwhelmed by our emotions. Whether it's anger, sadness, or anxiety, emotions can be powerful and overwhelming. But suppressing or ignoring our emotions can have serious consequences on our mental health, and it's important to learn how to process and release them in a healthy way.

When we suppress our emotions, they don't just disappear. They can build up and eventually lead to a breakdown or outburst. Emotions can also manifest themselves physically, leading to headaches, body aches, and other health issues.

Processing and releasing emotions is an essential part of emotional regulation and overall well-being. Although it may feel daunting to confront difficult emotions, finding the right techniques and methods can make the process more manageable.

There are many techniques and methods for processing and releasing emotions, and it's important to find what works best for you. Here are a few options to consider:

1. **Journaling:** By writing down your thoughts and emotions, you can gain insight into your inner workings and process them in a healthy way. Research has shown that journaling can reduce symptoms of depression, anxiety, and stress.

2. **Mindfulness meditation:** This practice involves focusing your attention on the present moment and observing your thoughts and emotions without judgment. Mindfulness meditation has been found to reduce symptoms of anxiety and depression and improve emotional regulation.

3. **Physical activity:** Physical activity is also a powerful tool for releasing emotions. Exercise and movement can help release pent-up emotions and improve your mood. Research has shown that physical activity can reduce symptoms of anxiety and depression and improve overall well-being.

4. **Creative expression:** Creative expression can also be a powerful outlet for processing and releasing emotions. Art, music, or dance can provide a creative and expressive way to process emotions that might be difficult to put into words.

5. **Seeking support:** Seeking support from a therapist, friend, or loved one can provide a safe and supportive space for working through your emotions. Talking to someone who is trained to help you process your

emotions can be a valuable tool in emotional regulation and overall well-being.

Emotional processing and release can have a number of positive benefits for our mental and physical well-being. These benefits include but are not limited to:

1. **Reduced stress and anxiety:** When we suppress or ignore our emotions, they can build up and cause a lot of stress and anxiety. By working through them, we can alleviate some of that pressure and help ourselves feel more calm and centered.

2. **Improved relationships:** When we're able to communicate our emotions more effectively, we can build stronger, more meaningful relationships with others. When we understand and respect our own emotions, we're better equipped to understand and respect the emotions of those around us.

3. **Better physical health:** Our emotions don't just affect our mental state; they can also have a physical impact on our bodies. For example, stress and anxiety can cause headaches, body aches, and other physical symptoms. By processing and releasing our emotions, we can reduce these physical symptoms and feel better overall.

4. **Increased self-awareness:** When we're in touch with our emotions and understand how they impact us, we're more self-aware and more confident in ourselves. We're better equipped to make decisions that are in line

with our values and goals, and we're more comfortable in our own skin.

Overall, emotional processing and release are critical skills for maintaining good mental health. By acknowledging and working through our emotions in healthy ways, we can build resilience and feel more in control of our lives.

LIFE HACKS FOR QUICK ANXIETY RELIEF

Feeling anxious is a common experience for many of us. Whether it's the pressure of a looming deadline or an upcoming event that makes us nervous, anxiety can be overwhelming and difficult to manage. When we overthink, we tend to amplify our anxiety, causing it to spiral out of control.

Fortunately, there are strategies that we can use to quickly reduce our anxiety and bring ourselves back to a state of calm. In this section, we'll explore some life hacks that you can use to help manage your anxiety in the moment.

Take a deep breath

One of the simplest ways to reduce anxiety is by taking a deep breath. When we're anxious, we tend to take short, shallow breaths, which can make the anxiety worse. Taking a deep breath can help slow down our heart rate and calm our nervous system.

To practice deep breathing, sit or stand up straight and take a slow, deep breath in through your nose. Hold your breath for three seconds, and then slowly exhale through your mouth. Repeat this process a few times until you start to feel calmer.

Practice progressive muscle relaxation

Progressive muscle relaxation is a technique that involves tensing and then relaxing different muscle groups in the body to help release tension and reduce anxiety.

To practice progressive muscle relaxation, start by tensing the muscles in your feet and holding the tension for three seconds. Then, release the tension and feel the muscles relax. Move on to your calves, thighs, and so on until you've tensed and relaxed every muscle group in your body. This technique can help you feel more relaxed and reduce your anxiety in just a few minutes.

Ground yourself in the present

When we're feeling anxious, our thoughts tend to race ahead, and we can feel like we're spiraling out of control. To combat this, it can be helpful to ground yourself in the present moment. Take a moment to notice your surroundings and focus on what's happening right now.

You can do this by looking around and naming the things you see or taking note of the sounds and sensations around you. This technique can help you feel more centered and in control, reducing your anxiety in the process.

THE IMPORTANCE OF PRACTICING SELF-CARE FOR ANXIETY MANAGEMENT

While there are many strategies that can help reduce anxiety in the moment, it's also important to focus on overall anxiety management. One key component of this is self-care. Taking care of your physical, emotional, and mental health can help build resilience and make you more capable of handling anxiety when it arises.

Here are some tips for practicing self-care for anxiety management:

1. **Get enough sleep:** Lack of sleep can increase anxiety and make it more difficult to manage. Aim for seven to nine hours of sleep each night.
2. **Eat a healthy diet:** What you eat can impact your mood and anxiety levels. Focus on a diet rich in whole foods, fruits, vegetables, and lean proteins.
3. **Exercise regularly:** Exercise is a great way to release tension and improve mood. Aim for at least 30 minutes of moderate exercise per day.
4. **Practice relaxation techniques:** Techniques like deep breathing, progressive muscle relaxation, and yoga can help calm the mind and body.
5. **Avoid caffeine and alcohol:** Both can increase anxiety and interfere with sleep, so it's best to limit or avoid them.

6. **Connect with others:** Social support can be a powerful tool for managing anxiety. Reach out to friends, family, or a support group.
7. **Set boundaries:** Overcommitting can increase stress and anxiety. Learn to say no and prioritize your own needs.
8. **Practice mindfulness:** Mindfulness practices like meditation, journaling, or mindful breathing can help reduce anxiety and build resilience.

By prioritizing self-care, you can build a strong foundation for managing anxiety in the long term.

Final thoughts

As we come to the end of this chapter on emotional mastery, I want to leave you with a final thought. Emotional regulation is not just a skill to be learned, but a journey to be lived. It's a process of self-discovery and growth, of learning to accept our emotions and use them to fuel positive change in our lives.

The techniques and strategies we've discussed in this chapter are only the beginning. They provide a foundation for emotional mastery, but the true work lies in practicing them consistently and making them a part of our daily lives.

Remember that emotional mastery is not about achieving a state of constant happiness or bliss. It's about learning to navigate the ups and downs of life with greater ease and resilience. It's about embracing the full range of human emotions and using them as tools to create a more meaningful and fulfilling life.

So, as you move forward on your journey of emotional mastery, I encourage you to approach it with an open mind and a compassionate heart. Be kind to yourself, and remember that growth is a process that takes time and effort. Celebrate your successes, learn from your challenges, and trust in your ability to create the life you want.

STEP 5

CALM DOWN FAST

Overthinking can be a source of immense stress, and the more we do it, the worse it can get. Our worries and concerns about the future can cloud our minds, preventing us from enjoying the present moment.

In the words of Randy Armstrong, "Worrying does not take away tomorrow's troubles; it takes away today's peace." Fortunately, there are simple, effective ways to calm down and find your way back to the present moment when you feel like your thoughts are spiraling out of control.

In this chapter, I'll explore some quick and easy techniques to reduce anxiety and manage stress, so you can find relief when overthinking has knocked you into a stressful state.

Buckle up, take a deep breath, and let's dive in!

THE FIGHT-FLIGHT RESPONSE

Overthinking can lead to a state of heightened anxiety that can be incredibly draining on both our mental and physical health. When we overthink, our minds become consumed with negative thoughts and worries, often centered around worst-case scenarios that may never come to pass. Unfortunately, this type of thinking can be incredibly destructive and can trigger the fight-flight response in our bodies.

The fight-flight response is a physiological reaction that occurs in response to perceived danger or threat. It's a survival mechanism that prepares the body to either combat danger or escape from it by releasing hormones like adrenaline and cortisol, increasing heart rate, and redirecting blood flow to major muscle groups. While the fight-flight response is critical in life-threatening situations, it can also be triggered in response to less severe stressors such as overthinking.

When we overthink, our bodies perceive a threat, and the fight-flight response is triggered. This response can make us feel anxious, tense, and on edge, leading to a wide range of negative physical and emotional symptoms. Additionally, overthinking can keep us stuck in a state of hyperarousal, making it difficult to calm down and relax, even when there is no immediate danger.

ACTIVATING THE PARASYMPATHETIC NERVOUS SYSTEM

When we have a thought that feels "dangerous," we often go straight into fight-or-flight mode, and our sympathetic nervous system is triggered, leading to symptoms like rapid heart rate, sweating, and shallow breathing. The fight-flight response is a natural reaction to perceived danger, but when we constantly engage in overthinking, our brain becomes accustomed to easily triggering this response and it creates a state of chronic stress. Fortunately, there are ways to counteract the fight-flight response and calm the body down quickly. One effective method is to engage the parasympathetic nervous system. The parasympathetic system is responsible for calming the body and reducing stress by slowing down the heart rate and breathing.

QUICK FIXES FOR REDUCING ANXIETY AND STRESS

If you're anything like me, you've had those moments where you're overwhelmed and anxious, and it feels like there's nothing you can do to calm down. In these situations, it's helpful to have some quick and effective strategies for reducing anxiety and stress. Here are a few strategies you can try when you need to calm down quickly in the moment:

Taking a dip in water

When you are feeling stressed and overwhelmed with over-thinking, there's nothing like taking a dip in a pool or hopping in the shower to help you relax. The soothing, flowing feeling of water can help distract your mind and engage your parasympathetic nervous system, which can counteract the fight-flight response triggered by overthinking. A study published in the International Journal of Stress Management found that taking a warm bath can significantly reduce symptoms of anxiety. So, next time you're feeling anxious, take a few minutes to soak in the tub or even turn on the shower for a few minutes of hot water therapy. The weightlessness of being submerged in water can stimulate the body's relaxation response, slowing down the heart rate and reducing muscle tension. Additionally, water can provide a sensory distraction, particularly if the temperature is slightly warmer or cooler than your body temperature. The sound of running water can also have a calming effect on the brain, particularly for people who are prone to overthinking or racing thoughts.

Rehydrating with water

Staying hydrated is important for overall health, but it can also have a calming effect on the body and mind. Rehydrating with a glass of water can help calm your breathing and heart rate while also providing a momentary distraction from overthinking. Taking a few moments to mindfully drink a glass of water can help maximize its calming effects. So if you're feeling anxious or overwhelmed, take a deep breath and sip on some cool water to help soothe your nerves. Dehydration can increase feelings of anxiety and stress, as the body's systems are not functioning at their best without adequate hydration. Drinking water can help to regulate the body's systems and reduce the effects of dehydration, allowing you to feel more relaxed and focused. Additionally, the act of taking a mindful moment to drink water can be meditative and calming, providing a brief respite from the busyness of the mind.

Spending time in nature

Nature has a healing effect on the body and mind, so simply getting outside for a walk or spending time in a park can help reduce anxiety and improve your mood. The sights, sounds, and smells of nature can help you feel more connected to the present moment, and being in natural environments has been shown to improve mental health. So, next time you're feeling stressed or overwhelmed, take a moment to step outside and immerse yourself in nature. Being in natural environments has been shown to reduce cortisol levels, a hormone associated with stress, and increase levels of serotonin, a hormone associated with positive mood. Additionally, natural environments can provide a sensory experience that engages the parasympathetic nervous system, which can help counteract the fight-flight response triggered by overthinking. Being in nature can also provide a mental break from the demands of daily life, allowing you to disconnect and recharge.

Engaging in a distracting activity

When your mind won't slow down, it can be hard to shift your focus and relax. Engaging in an activity that fully absorbs your attention can help distract your mind from overthinking and reduce anxiety. Watching a movie, listening to music, or singing are just a few examples of activities that can be used to take your mind off of your thoughts. Distracting activities can help you feel more relaxed and provide a mental break from your worries. From a scientific perspective, engaging in a distracting activity helps to shift the focus of the mind away from stressful thoughts, which can reduce the activation of the amygdala, the brain's fear center. This can lead to a decrease in the production of stress hormones like cortisol and an increase in the production of endorphins, the body's natural painkillers. The distraction also provides a mental break that can help interrupt the cycle of negative thoughts, giving your mind a chance to rest and reset.

Repeating a calming mantra

Repeating a calming mantra to yourself can provide a simple and effective way to reduce anxiety and stress. Some popular mantras to consider include, "This too shall pass," "I am safe and secure," and "Everything is working out for my highest good." Mantras can be said out loud or repeated silently to yourself, providing a sense of calm and reassurance. When you repeat a positive statement to yourself, it can help reframe your thoughts and emotions, and increase your confidence and self-esteem. This can help to counteract the negative self-talk that often accompanies anxiety and stress. Additionally, the act of repetition can also help to create a meditative state in the mind, which can have a calming effect on the body and reduce stress and anxiety.

Laugh

Laughter can have a powerful effect on the body, triggering the release of endorphins that can reduce stress and anxiety. So go ahead and watch a funny video, share a joke with a friend, or engage in any activity that makes you laugh. Laughter can also help shift your perspective and give your brain some much needed rest from worries. Laughter helps to reduce stress and anxiety by activating the release of endorphins. These endorphins produce a feeling of euphoria and can help to counteract the negative effects of stress and anxiety. Additionally, laughter also has a social bonding effect, which can help to reduce feelings of isolation and increase feelings of connectedness. This can have a positive effect on mental health and overall well-being.

Releasing excess adrenaline

Have you ever felt like you had too much bottled-up energy? Jumping or jogging in place can be a quick way to relieve stress and anxiety. It can also help you release excess adrenaline, which can build up in the body when you are stressed. Engaging in movement can provide a sense of control over your body and help clear your mind. When you engage in physical activity, your brain releases endorphins, which can elevate your mood and help you feel more relaxed. This is because exercise can trigger the parasympathetic nervous system, which can counteract the fight-flight response. To feel more grounded and centered when you're feeling stressed, try jumping or jogging in place for a few minutes.

Remember your successes

Sometimes we get so focused on the negative that we forget about the good things we have accomplished. That's when we need to remind ourselves of times when we have succeeded in the past. Compare the situation you're in right now to worse ones you have overcome before. This can help put things into perspective and remind you of your own resilience. When we experience anxiety, our minds can get stuck in a cycle of over-thinking. By shifting our perspective, we can break out of this cycle and gain a new sense of clarity. This is because when we engage in mindful reflection, we activate the prefrontal cortex, which can help regulate emotions and reduce stress.

Practicing deep belly breathing

Deep belly breathing is a simple and effective technique for reducing stress and anxiety. When we inhale deeply through our nose and let our bellies expand, we activate the parasympathetic nervous system, which can counteract the fight-flight response. Exhaling slowly through our mouths can then help us feel more relaxed and centered in the present moment.

Breathing exercises can also help regulate heart rate variability. This variability can indicate the health of our nervous system and is associated with emotional regulation. By practicing deep belly breathing, we can improve this and our ability to manage stress. So whenever you're feeling anxious, try taking a few deep breaths to help you feel more grounded and centered.

Acupressure

Acupressure is a traditional Chinese healing technique that involves applying pressure to specific points on the body to stimulate healing and reduce stress and anxiety. Common acupressure points for stress relief include the earlobes, the base of the skull, and the point between the eyebrows. Applying pressure to these points can help activate the body's natural healing response, leading to a reduction in stress and anxiety. Research has shown that acupressure can be an effective way to reduce anxiety. Acupressure stimulates the body's natural self-healing mechanisms, including the release of the body's natural painkillers, endorphins. By applying pressure to specific points, acupressure can help reduce muscle tension, calm the mind, and promote relaxation, all of which can help reduce stress and anxiety.

Crying

Crying can have a powerful effect on reducing stress and anxiety, allowing you to release pent-up emotions and find relief. In fact, research has shown that crying can stimulate the parasympathetic nervous system. So if you feel like crying, allow yourself the space and time to do so. Find a private space where you feel comfortable and safe, and let the tears flow. Crying helps release emotional buildup in the body, reducing the levels of stress hormones like cortisol. Crying also triggers the release of endorphins, which can help reduce pain and improve mood. Additionally, crying can help regulate breathing, heart rate, and blood pressure, all of which can help reduce anxiety. While crying may be seen as a sign of weakness by some, it is actually a natural and healthy way to release stress and anxiety, allowing you to find relief and move forward.

Creating or doing

Engaging in a creative or productive activity can provide a positive focus for your mind and help reduce anxiety. When your mind goes to overthinking mode, completing a task can give you a sense of control and safety in an otherwise stressful situation. It's a great way to take your mind off of negative thoughts and redirect your energy towards something positive. Tasks such as cooking, drawing, or cleaning can provide an outlet for your energy and help you feel productive. This can also help improve your sense of well-being and self-esteem. So take some time to engage in an activity that you find meaningful. You may find that doing something as simple as washing the dishes can provide a sense of relief and calm. Engaging in a creative or productive activity can also have physiological benefits. Studies have shown that engaging in creative activities can stimulate the release of dopamine, a neurotransmitter associated with feelings of pleasure and reward. When we feel good, our body is less likely to go into the fight-flight response, which can help reduce stress and anxiety. Engaging in creative activities can also have a meditative effect on the mind, allowing us to enter a state of flow where we become fully absorbed in the task at hand. This state of flow can help reduce stress and anxiety by providing a mental break from overthinking and promoting a sense of calm and relaxation.

PERSONAL STORIES OF USING QUICK FIXES

Finding ways to calm down and destress can be a personal journey, but sometimes hearing about how others have used quick fixes to reduce anxiety can help you find what works for you. So cozy up; it's story time!

Sarah found herself in the middle of an intense work meeting that triggered a wave of anxiety. She excused herself and went to the bathroom, where she splashed cold water on her face, took deep breaths, and reminded herself that it was just a meeting. When she returned, she felt more calm and collected and was able to finish the meeting with a clear mind.

Jonathan found himself unable to fall asleep at night due to his anxiety. He decided to try a calming mantra and repeated "I am safe and secure" to himself until he drifted off to sleep. This allowed him to bypass his racing thoughts and focus on a calming phrase, helping him get some much-needed rest.

The examples of personal stories are endless, and each one highlights the uniqueness of their own personal experiences. Whether it's taking a dip in the tub, doing a belly breathing exercise, or simply laughing at a silly joke, quick fixes can have a powerful impact on reducing anxiety and stress. People from all walks of life have found success with these strategies, including athletes, celebrities, and everyday individuals.

Final thoughts

Now that you have a variety of tools in your toolbox for managing stress and anxiety, it's time to put them into action. Remember, managing stress and anxiety is an ongoing process, and what works for one person may not work for another. So be patient with yourself as you explore different strategies and find what works best for you. It's also important to remember that quick fixes are just that – temporary solutions for immediate relief. For long-term management of stress and anxiety, it's important to address the root causes of your stress and develop healthy coping mechanisms. This may involve seeking professional help or making lifestyle changes, such as improving your sleep or reducing your workload. By taking action and proactively managing your stress and anxiety, you can improve your overall well-being and lead a happier, healthier life. So take the first step today and try out one of the quick fixes mentioned in this guide. You never know – it could be just what you need to calm down and destress. In the next chapter, I'll take a closer look at the importance of self-care and explore some effective strategies for making self-care a priority in your life. It's important to remember that while quick fixes can provide temporary relief from stress and anxiety, it's essential to prioritize self-care as a long-term solution for maintaining good mental health. So let's dive in and learn how to take care of ourselves in a way that promotes inner peace and well-being.

STEP 6

SLEEP IT OFF

As we've seen throughout this book, overthinking can take a serious toll on our mental and physical health. It can leave us feeling drained, stressed, and anxious. That's why it's so important to take steps to build our resilience and give ourselves the tools we need to manage overthinking when it arises. And one of the most powerful tools we have is sleep.

It's easy to overlook the importance of sleep, especially when we're busy and stressed. But the truth is that sleep is absolutely vital to our overall health and well-being. Without enough quality sleep, it's almost impossible to function well at all. In fact, sleep is even more important to our physical and mental health than diet and exercise.

But what exactly is it about sleep that makes it so crucial to our resilience? In this chapter, we'll explore the ways in which sleep affects our brains, our bodies, and our emotional well-being. We'll look at the latest scientific research on sleep and mental health, and I'll offer practical tips and strategies for getting the restful, restorative sleep we all need to thrive. So put on your pajamas, fluff up your pillow, and get ready to learn about the power of sleep.

SLEEP, YOUR BRAIN, AND MENTAL HEALTH

Sleep is something we all crave after a long day of work, but did you know that it does more than just make you feel rested and rejuvenated? It actually has a profound impact on our brain and mental health. One of the key aspects of sleep that is important to our mental well-being is REM sleep.

REM sleep, which is one of the stages of the sleep cycle, fine-tunes our emotional circuits and fuels creativity. It allows us to process and make sense of the events of the day. Without enough REM sleep, we may experience mood swings and find it difficult to manage our emotions.

In addition to emotional processing, sleep also has an important impact on learning and memory. During sleep, the brain frees up space for new memories and helps us remember new information. It's like giving our brain the opportunity to file away all the new information we've learned during the day, making it easier to retrieve later.

Sleep also plays a housekeeping role in our brain, as it removes toxins that build up from when we are awake. This house-keeping function is essential to our brain's health and function-ality. Without enough quality sleep, we may be putting our brains at risk for long-term health problems.

Sleep plays a crucial role in regulating our bodies and keeping them healthy. It impacts not only our physical health but also our cognitive abilities. When we don't get enough quality sleep, our higher cortical functions, such as multitasking, attention, and problem-solving, can become compromised. This can make it more difficult for us to perform at our best. Additionally, sleep deprivation has been linked to depression, and research shows that people who suffer from depression often have a compromised circadian rhythm.

The circadian rhythm is a natural, internal process that regulates the sleep-wake cycle and other physiological processes that occur throughout the day. It is controlled by a part of the brain called the suprachiasmatic nucleus, which responds to external cues such as light and dark to keep our bodies in sync with the day-night cycle.

Disruptions to our circadian rhythm, such as those caused by poor sleep habits or changes in our work schedule, can have a significant impact on our physical and mental health. Therefore, if you're feeling down or struggling with cognitive tasks, it's important to make sure you're getting enough quality sleep and maintaining a regular sleep-wake cycle to support your circadian rhythm.

Insomnia is also a major cause of anxiety and depression, and people who suffer from it are many more times likely to have these conditions. If you find that you're having trouble sleeping, it may be helpful to try some of the sleep-promoting strategies I'll discuss later in this chapter.

SLEEP AND YOUR BODY

Getting enough quality sleep is not just essential for mental well-being, but for physical health as well. Sleep helps our bodies to rest and rejuvenate, which is essential for maintaining optimal health. Our muscles, for example, need time to relax and recover from daily wear and tear. Without enough quality sleep, our muscles and bodies can feel weak and depleted.

In fact, research has shown that the impact of sleep on physical health goes beyond just muscle recovery. The sleep-wake cycle has an important impact on all organ systems in the body, and a lack of sleep has been linked to a number of physical diseases and disorders. Studies have found that poor sleep quality can affect weight, blood sugar levels, and even longevity.

While the exact mechanism behind the connection between sleep and physical health is not fully understood, research suggests that sleep plays a crucial role in regulating our bodies and keeping them healthy. So, next time you feel tempted to stay up late binge-watching your favorite show, remember that getting enough quality sleep is crucial for both your mind and body.

HOW MUCH SLEEP DO YOU NEED?

Ah, sleep—the thing we all know we need but never seem to get enough of. While most of us have a vague idea of how many hours of sleep we should be getting each night, the truth is that there is no one-size-fits-all answer when it comes to sleep needs. Everyone is different, and our sleep needs can even vary throughout our lives.

That being said, there are some general guidelines that can help you determine how much sleep you need. For example, babies initially sleep for as much as 16 to 18 hours per day, which may boost growth and development (especially of the brain). School-age children and teenagers, on average, need about 9.5 hours of sleep per night. Most adults need 7-9 hours of sleep a night, but this can vary depending on your own natural biorhythms.

The best way to figure out how much sleep you need is to pay attention to how you feel throughout the day. If you feel rested and alert during the day, you're probably getting enough sleep. If you feel sluggish or tired, you may need to adjust your sleep schedule to get more rest. One way to figure out your own sleep cycle is to use a sleep tracker app, which can help you identify patterns in your sleep and wake cycles and track how much REM sleep you are getting.

HOW TO SLEEP BETTER

A good night's sleep is essential for a resilient life. The question is, how do you ensure you get one? If you're struggling to get some quality shuteye, here are a few tips to help you sleep better:

Establish a sleep routine

One of the best ways to ensure a good night's sleep is to establish a sleep routine. Go to bed and wake up at the same time every day. This helps your body establish a natural sleep rhythm, which can make it easier to fall asleep and wake up feeling rested.

Relaxation techniques before bed

There are plenty of things that can help you relax before bed. Activities such as meditation, reading, light stretching, or listening to calming music can help put your mind at ease and prepare you for sleep. If you're looking for something a bit more invigorating, consider taking a warm bath or shower before bed. The hot water helps change your body's core temperature so that you go to bed with a lower temperature, which can help you fall asleep more easily.

Try a brain dump

A brain dump is a technique that involves writing down all of your thoughts, worries, and to-do items before going to bed. The idea is to empty your mind of all the mental clutter that can keep you up at night. By getting everything out of your head and onto paper, you free up mental space and reduce the chance of racing thoughts and anxiety. This technique can be particularly helpful for people who tend to overthink or have trouble relaxing at night.

After completing a brain dump, it's important to physically put the notebook or paper away and tell yourself that you'll address those thoughts and tasks tomorrow. This helps to create a mental boundary between your thoughts and your sleep, reducing the chance of rumination and anxiety. By taking this step, you signal to your brain that it's time to let go of the day's worries and prepare for restful sleep.

Cutting back on certain kinds of light

The blue light emitted by electronic devices can disrupt your sleep cycle by suppressing the production of melatonin, the hormone that regulates sleep. So, try to avoid screens for at least an hour before bed, and use the blue-light filter setting on your phone or tablet (this is commonly called "night mode") to reduce the amount of blue light that reaches your eyes.

Aromatherapy oil diffusers for a relaxing scent

Aromatherapy can help you relax and drift off to sleep. Essential oils like lavender, chamomile, and clary sage can help you fall asleep more easily and sleep more soundly.

Getting out of bed if you can't sleep

Staying in bed while unable to sleep can actually make the problem worse. This is because our brains begin to associate the bed with frustration and sleeplessness, which can make it even harder to fall asleep in the future. It's better to get up and do something else until you feel tired again, and then return to bed.

This helps reestablish the association between bed and sleep, which can help promote more restful sleep in the long run. So, if you find yourself tossing and turning in bed and can't sleep, it's best to get up and do something calming until you feel ready to try sleeping again. Reading a book or listening to calming music are good options because they don't involve bright screens or stimulating activities that could interfere with sleep.

By following these tips, you can create a relaxing evening wind-down routine that helps prepare you for a good night's sleep.

READY, SET, SLEEP: CREATING YOUR IDEAL EVENING WIND-DOWN ROUTINE

Now that you have the tools and techniques to enable you to sleep better, it's time to put all this newfound knowledge to use and create an evening wind-down routine that will help you catch those elusive zzz's.

So, grab a notebook and pen, or your phone, and start brainstorming. Remember, everyone's routine is different, so don't worry if yours looks nothing like your partner's or friend's. I'll give you an example of a wind-down routine. You can take this as a starting point to make one that is your own. It's all about finding what works best for you.

- 8:00 PM - Turn off all electronics to begin winding down for the night.
- 8:15 PM - Take a warm bath or shower to relax your body and mind.
- 8:30 PM - Light a lavender-scented candle or use an essential oil diffuser with lavender oil to promote relaxation.

- 8:45 PM - Do some light stretching or gentle yoga poses to release any tension in your muscles.
- 9:00 PM - Read a book or listen to calming music to help you wind down.
- 9:30 PM - Write in a gratitude journal to reflect on the positive things in your life.
- 9:45 PM - Practice some deep breathing exercises or meditation to calm your mind.
- 10:00 PM - Turn off the lights and get ready for some well-deserved rest.

Remember, the goal of an evening wind-down routine is to create a peaceful and calming environment that signals to your mind and body that it's time for sleep. It's important to be consistent with your routine, so your body knows what to expect and can start to relax and wind down naturally.

Now it's your turn to create a routine that works best for you! Don't forget to make it your own and have fun with it. Sweet dreams!

Final thoughts

We've covered a lot of ground so far when it comes to over-thinking, and I hope you've found some helpful tips and strategies to help you manage it.

Remember, overthinking is something that we all struggle with from time to time, and there's no one-size-fits-all solution. But by combining some of the quick fixes we've discussed, such as mindfulness, exercise, and acupressure, with some of the more long-term strategies like therapy, gratitude, and sleep, you can start to build up your resilience and become better equipped to handle the challenges that come your way.

It's important to give yourself grace and space as you work on managing your overthinking. Change doesn't happen overnight, so be patient with yourself and celebrate the small wins along the way. And most importantly, remember that you're not alone in this – there are millions of people out there who struggle with overthinking just like you do.

So take a deep breath, and let's move on to the next chapter, where I'll tackle another common form of overthinking: indecision and analysis paralysis.

STEP 7

WHAT TO DO?

Theodore Roosevelt once said, "In a moment of decision, the best thing you can do is the right thing to do, the next best thing is the wrong thing, and the worst thing you can do is nothing." And isn't it true? Indecision and analysis paralysis can lead us down a path of stress and worry, leaving us feeling stuck and frozen. In this chapter, I'll explore how to make decisions that are right for you and learn how to take action when you need to.

Whether it's deciding on what to eat for dinner or whether to quit your job and start your own business, decision-making is an essential part of life. It's also important to note that making decisions and taking action go hand-in-hand. Even if we make the wrong decision, taking action can often be more beneficial than doing nothing at all. So, let's explore the art of decision-making and how we can get unstuck and take action when we need to.

GETTING UNSTUCK

Do you ever feel stuck in life? It's like being in quicksand; the more you struggle, the deeper you sink. It can be frustrating, and sometimes, it feels like you are going nowhere. But here's the thing: you're not alone. We all go through periods where we feel stuck, indecisive, and unsure of what to do next.

Defining what it means to be stuck is essential for identifying when we are, in fact, stuck. Being stuck can come in many forms and affect different aspects of our lives. Some common signs that we might be stuck include:

- Feeling unmotivated
- Struggling to make decisions
- Avoiding taking action
- Feeling disconnected or unfulfilled
- Feeling like we're in a rut

Being stuck can manifest in different ways: it could be analysis paralysis, where you're overthinking and can't decide on what to do, or it could be a feeling of being trapped in a job, relationship, or situation. Whatever form it takes, being stuck is not a fun place to be.

1. Take action

When you're feeling stuck, taking any action is better than taking no action at all. The fear of failure can often prevent us from taking the first step, but remember that it's better to try and fail than to not try at all. Identify one small step you can take to move forward and take action. This could be something as simple as sending an email or making a phone call. Once you've taken that first step, it can be easier to keep going and make progress.

Another way to take action is to break down your goals into smaller, manageable tasks. This can make them feel less overwhelming and more achievable. Start by identifying the smallest possible action you can take, and build from there. Celebrate your progress along the way, and remember that every step, no matter how small, is moving you closer to your goal.

2. Gain clarity

When you're feeling stuck, it can be helpful to gain clarity on what you want and what's important to you. Take some time to reflect on your values, passions, and goals. Ask yourself what you want to achieve, and why it's important to you. Visualize what success looks like and imagine how it will feel when you achieve it. Having a clear vision can help you stay focused and motivated.

One way to gain clarity is to create a vision board or write out your goals. This can help you visualize your dreams and make them feel more real. You can also try journaling or talking to a trusted friend or mentor about your goals. Sometimes, just putting your thoughts and ideas down on paper can help clarify what you want and what you need to do to achieve it.

3. Get an outside perspective

Talking to someone you trust and respect can help you gain a different perspective on your situation. This person may have insights or ideas that you hadn't considered before. They may also be able to provide encouragement and support. When seeking an outside perspective, be sure to choose someone who has your best interests at heart and who will be honest with you.

Another way to do this is to read or listen to books, podcasts, or other resources that are relevant to your situation. This can help you see your situation in a new light and provide ideas and inspiration for moving forward.

4. Identify limiting beliefs

Limiting beliefs are thoughts that hold us back from achieving our goals. They can be self-defeating and prevent us from taking action. Identifying these beliefs is the first step in breaking free from them. Ask yourself what beliefs are holding you back. Write them down and challenge them. Ask yourself if they are really true or if they are just assumptions.

One way to challenge limiting beliefs is to reframe them. Instead of thinking, "I'm not good enough," try reframing it to "I'm capable of learning and growing." This can help shift your mindset from one of limitation to one of possibility.

5. Let go of the need for control

It's natural to want to have control over our lives, but sometimes the desire for control can become overwhelming and cause more stress than it's worth. Learning to let go of the need for control can be liberating and lead to a more peaceful existence.

Trusting that things will work out as they should can allow you to focus on what you can control and let go of what you can't. This can lead to better decision-making, improved relationships, and a more positive outlook on life.

6. Embrace change

Change is a fundamental part of life and can bring about new opportunities, growth, and learning. However, it can also be scary and overwhelming. It's important to remember that change can be an opportunity for personal and professional growth.

Embracing change requires a shift in mindset and a willingness to step out of your comfort zone. By approaching change with a positive attitude, you can create new experiences, learn new skills, and achieve your goals. Remember, the only constant in life is change, so it's important to learn how to adapt and thrive in any situation.

7. Be kind to yourself

We often put a lot of pressure on ourselves to be perfect, to achieve all our goals, and to be everything to everyone. However, this pressure can lead to negative self-talk and self-criticism, which can be damaging to our mental and emotional well-being. Being kind to yourself means treating yourself with compassion and empathy and accepting yourself for who you are.

It involves acknowledging your strengths and weaknesses and giving yourself permission to make mistakes. By practicing self-kindness, you can build resilience, improve your relationships, and increase your overall happiness and well-being. Remember, you are deserving of kindness and love, and it all starts with how you treat yourself.

HOW MUCH INFORMATION DO YOU NEED?

When it comes to deciding something, it's important to gather enough information to make a good decision. But when we take it too far and find ourselves researching every single possible little detail, we end up with so much information that it becomes impossible to make a decision. This is called analysis paralysis. It happens when we think that, after all, the more information we have, the more confident we can be that our choice was the right one. To a point, yes, this is true. You shouldn't jump into any big decision without knowing infor-mation about it. But there is such a thing as having too much information, and when you get to that point, you can throw all hope of making the "best" decision out the window because you won't be able to make any decision at all.

So how do you know when you've gathered enough information to make a decision? It can be difficult to determine, but I have some very helpful methods you can use to make any decision much more manageable.

One strategy is to establish a set of criteria or priorities to guide your decision-making. This can help you identify what is most important and make more informed choices. Break down your decision into smaller, more manageable parts. This can make the decision feel less overwhelming and help you focus on the key factors that will drive the outcome.

In addition to these strategies, it can be helpful to take a step back and examine the situation from a different perspective. This might involve temporarily removing yourself from the situation or considering the decision from someone else's point of view. Seeking out feedback and advice from others can also help you gain a fresh perspective and make more informed decisions.

Ultimately, it's important to remember that there is no one "right" way to make decisions and that what works best for one person may not work for another. By staying open-minded and exploring different approaches, you can find the strategies that work best for you and help you overcome analysis paralysis.

HOW TO MAKE GOOD DECISIONS

Making decisions can be difficult, but it doesn't have to be. Understanding the decision-making process can help you make better decisions that align with your goals and values.

It's helpful to understand the process of decision-making. According to research, decision-making involves several stages, including:

1. **Identifying the problem:** The first stage of decision-making involves identifying the problem or issue that needs to be addressed. It may seem silly to even mention this one because it seems like it should be obvious. But this first step is very important because if you don't start out with clearly identifying what is wrong, you may end up spending a lot of time and energy "fixing" something that was not actually the real problem.

2. **Gathering information:** Once the problem has been identified, the next step is to gather information about the problem. This may involve conducting research, consulting with experts, or gathering data to help inform the decision-making process.

3. **Evaluating the options:** After gathering information, it's important to evaluate the different options available. This may involve weighing the pros and cons of each option, considering the potential risks and benefits, and assessing the feasibility of each option.

4. **Making a choice:** Once the options have been evaluated, it's time to make a decision. This may involve choosing the option that best aligns with your goals and values, or selecting the option that has the greatest likelihood of success.

5. **Taking action:** The final stage of decision-making involves taking action to implement the chosen option. This may involve developing a plan, allocating resources, and taking steps to ensure that the decision is effectively executed.

By following these stages, you can make informed decisions that will lead to successful outcomes.

HOW TO BE SATISFIED WITH YOUR DECISIONS

Making decisions can be difficult, but it's important to remember that you have the power to make choices that will positively impact your life. It's easy to get caught up in second-guessing or regretting past decisions, but it's important to focus on the present and future. You are capable of making good decisions, and each decision you make is an opportunity to learn and grow.

It will help you to be satisfied with your decisions when you remember that every choice you make helps shape who you are and who you want to become. Even if a decision doesn't turn out as planned, it's an opportunity to learn from your mistakes and make better decisions in the future. Remember that failure is not the end result, but rather a stepping stone to success.

It's also important to recognize that making decisions can be empowering and satisfying in and of itself. The act of decision-making can be liberating and can give you a sense of accomplishment. Whether it's deciding to take a new job, move to a new city, or end a toxic relationship, making the decision to take action can be a huge weight off your shoulders.

Of course, not every decision will be perfect, and it's important to remember that perfection is not the goal. Instead, focus on making decisions that are aligned with your values and goals. Trust yourself and your intuition, and remember that you have the ability to make the best decision for yourself in any given situation.

Finally, it's important to celebrate your decisions, both big and small. Every decision you make, no matter how small, is a step forward in your life. Take the time to acknowledge and celebrate each decision you make, as it is a reflection of your own personal growth and development.

I understand that it can be challenging to make a decision, but it's important to remember that you are capable of making good choices that positively impact your life. Embrace the power of decision-making, learn from your mistakes, and celebrate your successes along the way. With each decision you make, you are taking control of your life and shaping your future into something bright and beautiful.

SUCCESS STORIES

Personal stories of successful decision-making can provide valuable insight and inspiration. For example, consider the story of Lena who went back to school in her 40's so she could switch career paths, despite the uncertainty and risks. By following her passion and taking calculated risks, she was able to work in a new field where she now makes more money and lives a more fulfilling life.

Another example is the story of Jake, who made the difficult decision to end a toxic relationship, despite the emotional pain and uncertainty. By prioritizing his own well-being and making a tough decision, he was able to move on and find a healthier relationship.

Overcome your fears

Have you ever felt paralyzed by fear? Maybe you want to change careers, but the fear of failure keeps you stuck in a job you hate. Or perhaps you're afraid of speaking in public, so you turn down opportunities to share your knowledge and ideas. Fear can be a powerful emotion that keeps us from reaching our full potential, but there are ways to overcome it.

One technique that has gained popularity in recent years is the fear-setting exercise, developed by Tim Ferriss. The purpose of this exercise is to identify and confront our fears by breaking them down into manageable pieces.

To complete the fear-setting exercise, follow these steps:

1. **Define the fear:** Write down the fear that is holding you back. This can be a fear of failure, rejection, or anything else that is preventing you from taking action.
2. **Determine the worst-case scenario:** Imagine the worst possible outcome of your fear coming true. What is the absolute worst thing that could happen? Write it down.
3. **Identify ways to prevent the worst-case scenario:** Consider what you could do to prevent the worst-case scenario from happening. Are there any steps you could take to reduce the likelihood of it happening?
4. **Determine the cost of inaction:** What would be the cost of doing nothing and letting your fear hold you back? How would your life be impacted if you continued to do nothing?
5. **Identify the benefits of taking action:** Consider the benefits of taking action and overcoming your fear. What positive outcomes could result from facing your fear?
6. **Develop a plan of action:** Based on your analysis, develop a plan of action to confront your fear and move forward.

If you're still not convinced, here are some personal stories of people who have used the fear-setting exercise to overcome their fears and achieve their goals:

Sarah had always dreamed of starting her own business but was too afraid to take the leap. She was worried about failing, losing money, and not being able to support herself. After hearing about the fear-setting exercise, she decided to give it a try. She listed all of her fears, the worst-case scenarios, and the steps she could take to prevent them from happening. She realized that the benefits of starting her own business outweighed the risks, and she finally took the plunge. Her business is now thriving, and she is living her dream.

John wanted to travel the world but was held back by his fear of flying. He tried everything from therapy to medication, but nothing seemed to work. One day, he stumbled upon the fear-setting exercise and decided to give it a try. He listed all of his fears and the steps he could take to prevent them from happening. He realized that the worst-case scenario was unlikely to happen and that the benefits of traveling far outweighed his fear. He booked a flight and took his first trip. He still gets nervous when he flies, but he now knows how to manage his fear and doesn't let it hold him back.

Michelle was stuck in a dead-end job and was too afraid to look for something better. She was worried about rejection, failure, and the unknown. She listed all of her fears, the worst-case scenarios, and the steps she could take to prevent them from happening. She realized that the benefits of finding a new job outweighed the risks, and she finally started looking. She landed a job she loves, and her career has taken off. She credits the fear-setting exercise for giving her the push she needed to take the first step.

Final thoughts

When it comes to managing stress and overcoming anxiety, taking action and making decisions are crucial. By understanding the decision-making process and practicing risk analysis and contingency planning, you can gain the confidence and clarity needed to move forward.

However, even with these tools and strategies, it's common to experience overwhelm and indecision at times. In the next chapter, I will explore practical tips and techniques for navigating these challenging moments and finding a sense of calm and control in the midst of stress.

STEP 8

GET OVER THE OVERWHELM

Are you feeling overwhelmed with life's challenges and struggling to keep up with the pace of your daily routine? You're not alone. Many of us experience a sense of helplessness when we are continually overthinking everything. The good news is there's a way to overcome this mental state and reclaim your life. In this chapter, I'll explore the causes of mental overwhelm and discuss effective strategies to help you manage it.

Mental overwhelm is a state of emotional and mental exhaustion where an individual feels that they have reached their limit and are unable to cope with the demands of daily life. It's a common experience that affects people of all ages and backgrounds. When you're feeling overwhelmed, it can be tough to think and act rationally and even function in a normal way. Mental overwhelm can manifest itself in many forms, including anxiety, depression, panic attacks, and physical symptoms such as fatigue, headaches, and muscle tension.

WARNING SIGNS

Have you ever felt like your life is just too complicated? It's a common feeling. The modern world is filled with an endless stream of information and distractions, making it difficult to navigate daily life without feeling overwhelmed. And when that overwhelm builds up, it can lead to a mental breakdown.

According to a Medium article, the modern world has become too complex for any of us to truly understand. Our society is filled with intricate systems, technologies, and social constructs that can be difficult to keep up with. It's no wonder that so many of us feel overwhelmed on a regular basis.

But it's not just external factors that contribute to our overwhelm. We also tend to make our lives more complicated than they need to be. When we overcommit or say yes to everything, we often add to our own overwhelm. Recognizing the signs of an impending breakdown is a crucial step in avoiding a mental health crisis. In addition to changes in sleep patterns, anxiety, and feelings of hopelessness, there are several other potential warning signs to watch out for. According to a study published in BMC Medicine, factors such as a high workload and a lack of support from colleagues and loved ones can increase the risk of a breakdown. Cleveland Clinic, one of the top-rated hospitals in the United States, offers some additional signs to look out for, including changes in appetite, memory loss, and an inability to concentrate.

It's essential to take note of these signs and to take action before it's too late. As the old saying goes, an ounce of prevention is worth a pound of cure. So, if you're experiencing any of these signs or symptoms, it's important to take a step back, evaluate your situation, and seek help if necessary. Remember, there's no shame in asking for help. Seeking the help of a mental health professional can be an incredibly beneficial step in overcoming overwhelm and preventing a mental health crisis.

DEPRESSURIZING: HOW TO CREATE IMMEDIATE EASE

Feeling overwhelmed is a common experience that many people face in their lives. However, by taking simple steps to depressurize, you can ease your stress levels and regain a sense of control. One helpful strategy is the 4 D's of time management: drop, defer, delegate, or do. The idea is to go through your to-do list and categorize each item into one of these four buckets:

Drop it: Eliminating unnecessary tasks

- Take inventory of your to-do list and identify items that aren't critical to your goals or well-being. Eliminating these tasks can free up valuable time and reduce mental clutter.
- Consider the 80/20 rule, which states that 80% of our results come from 20% of our efforts. By focusing on the most important tasks, we can maximize our

productivity while reducing the burden of nonessential tasks.

Defer it: Delaying non-urgent tasks

- Some tasks can be postponed until a later time, allowing you to focus on more pressing matters in the present moment. Determine which tasks can wait and reschedule them for a more convenient time.
- Prioritize your to-do list and tackle the most critical tasks first. This can help reduce anxiety and provide a sense of accomplishment as you work through your list.

Delegate it: Sharing responsibilities with others

- Not all tasks have to be completed by you alone. Consider which tasks can be delegated to others who may be better equipped to handle them or have more time available.
- Consider the benefits of collaboration and teamwork. By working with others, you can share the burden of tasks and benefit from diverse perspectives and skill sets.

Do it: Tackling tasks head-on

- Some tasks cannot be deferred or delegated and must be tackled head-on.
- Consider the benefits of breaking down large tasks into smaller, more manageable steps. This can help reduce

feelings of overwhelm and provide a sense of progress
and accomplishment as you work towards completing
the task.

Procrastination can lead to further overwhelm, so a good
strategy for reducing stress is to do things now. This is often
easier said than done, but research shows that taking action
quickly can help us avoid overthinking and second-guessing
ourselves.

One way to help you do things now is to break down larger
tasks into smaller, more manageable ones. This makes the
task seem less daunting and can help you take action more
easily. Additionally, setting deadlines for yourself can help
you stay accountable and ensure that you don't put off important tasks.

LESS IS MORE

Simplifying our lives can help reduce overwhelm and anxiety.
When we focus on what is truly important to us, we are better
able to identify what is worth our time and energy, and what
isn't.

One way to simplify life is to declutter our physical and mental
space. This includes getting rid of physical possessions that no
longer serve us, and also reducing mental clutter by limiting
our exposure to negative news or social media.

Another way to simplify is to focus on our priorities and elimi-
nate distractions. This means saying no to things that are not

aligned with our goals, and setting boundaries to protect our time and energy.

Overall, by simplifying our lives and managing our time better, we can reduce overwhelm and anxiety and achieve our goals more efficiently.

PERSONAL STORIES

Overcoming overwhelm can seem daunting, but hearing personal stories of others who have navigated these challenges can be inspiring and provide a sense of hope. Here are three stories of individuals who have overcome overwhelm and achieved their goals:

Sarah had always dreamed of opening her own bakery. She had a passion for baking and loved creating unique desserts for her family and friends. However, when it came to actually opening her own business, Sarah felt overwhelmed and unsure of where to start. She was working full-time and taking care of her young children, and the thought of adding a new venture to her plate seemed impossible. But Sarah refused to give up on her dream. She started small, baking for friends and family on the weekends and testing out new recipes. As she gained more confidence, she began to research what it would take to open her own bakery. With the help of a mentor and a solid plan, Sarah was able to quit her full-time job and open her own successful bakery.

Alex was a college student struggling with overwhelming anxiety. He found himself constantly worrying about his grades, his future, and his relationships. It became difficult for him to even leave his dorm room, let alone attend class or socialize with his friends. Alex sought the help of a therapist, who suggested he start small by setting achievable goals each day. Alex started with something as simple as going for a walk or attending one class. As he gained confidence, he began to take on more challenges, like joining a club on campus or volunteering at a local organization. With the help of his therapist and his own determination, Alex was able to overcome his anxiety and lead a more fulfilling college experience.

Maya was a working mom of two young children who felt like she was constantly drowning in her responsibilities. She had a demanding job, a busy household to manage, and little time for self-care. Maya realized that in order to overcome her overwhelm, she needed to prioritize her own well-being. She started by setting aside time each day for exercise and meditation, even if it was just for a few minutes. She also learned to delegate tasks to her partner and children, allowing her to have more time for herself. By taking small steps towards a more balanced life, Maya was able to reduce her stress and find more joy in her daily routine.

These personal stories demonstrate that no matter how overwhelming life can seem, it is possible to overcome these challenges and achieve your goals. By starting small, seeking support when needed, and prioritizing self-care, it is possible to navigate overwhelm and create a more fulfilling life.

Final thoughts

In this chapter, I've explored the causes and effects of mental overwhelm, as well as strategies for managing it. We've learned that complexity is often at the root of our overwhelm and that taking small steps and simplifying our lives can help alleviate the pressure. Additionally, we've heard personal stories of individuals who have overcome overwhelming situations and achieved their goals. It's important to remember that overwhelm is a natural response to stress and that by taking proactive steps, we can mitigate its negative impact and regain control.

In order to prevent overwhelm from taking over our lives, it's important to be kind to ourselves. We often place too much pressure on ourselves to be perfect, and this can lead to burnout and increased stress. In the next chapter, I will explore the importance of self-compassion and strategies for practicing self-kindness. By learning to treat ourselves with compassion and understanding, we can create a more positive and fulfilling life.

As you come to the end of this chapter, take a moment to appreciate how far you've come. You've gained insight into the roots of overthinking and learned strategies for regulating your emotions and thoughts. You've identified limiting beliefs and explored techniques for reframing them. And most importantly, you've learned to be kind to yourself and trust in your own ability to navigate life's ups and downs.

It's important to remember that change is a journey, and there may be times when you feel like you're taking two steps forward and one step back. But with the tools and strategies you've gained in this chapter, you'll be able to keep moving forward with confidence and resilience.

Remember to take small steps, stay present in the moment, and celebrate your progress along the way. By focusing on what you can control and letting go of what you can't, you'll be well on your way to living a fulfilling and joyous life.

STEP 9

PRACTICE MAITRI

Maitri, a Pali word, is commonly translated as love or loving-kindness. However, it also means loving-kindness to oneself. In other words, it's about treating yourself with the same love, kindness, forgiveness, and understanding that you give to those you love. Maitri is about cultivating a sense of deep compassion and respect for yourself, as well as others.

Self-love and kindness are important because they are the foundation of a healthy and fulfilling life. When we treat ourselves with love and kindness, we are better able to handle life's challenges and navigate difficult situations. We become more resilient and better equipped to deal with stress, anxiety, and depression.

Self-love and kindness also help us to establish healthy boundaries and to recognize our own worth and value. When we treat ourselves with love and respect, we are less likely to allow others to mistreat us or to compromise our own needs and desires.

When we practice self-love and kindness, we become more compassionate and understanding toward others. We are less judgmental and more forgiving of their mistakes and short-comings. This, in turn, can lead to more harmonious and fulfilling relationships, both in our personal and professional lives.

On the other hand, when we are harsh and critical towards ourselves, we are more likely to project those negative feelings onto others. This can lead to misunderstandings, conflicts, and a lack of trust in our relationships.

STRATEGIES FOR SELF-LOVE

For many of us, practicing self-love and kindness can be easier said than done. We may struggle with feelings of guilt, shame, or unworthiness or may have a hard time prioritizing our own needs.

In this section, I'll explore some practical strategies for practicing self-love and kindness based on research and expert advice. These strategies can help you cultivate a more positive and compassionate relationship with yourself and, ultimately, reduce the amount of time you spend overthinking.

Prioritizing self-care needs

Taking care of ourselves is often a last priority, especially when we have a lot of responsibilities or obligations. We tend to think that putting our needs first is selfish, but the truth is that neglecting our own needs can lead to burnout, anxiety, and depression. By paying attention to our emotional, physical, spiritual, and mental needs, we can improve our well-being and become more resilient.

To prioritize self-care, start by making a list of your needs in each of these areas. This might include getting enough sleep, eating nutritious food, spending time with loved ones, engaging in activities that bring you joy, or attending therapy. Then, rank these needs in order of importance and make a plan to meet them. This might involve saying no to certain requests, delegating tasks to others, or scheduling time in your calendar to prioritize self-care activities.

Talking kindly to yourself

It's easy to fall into the trap of negative self-talk, especially when we make mistakes or face challenges. But this kind of self-talk can be harmful and prevent us from reaching our full potential. To break the cycle of negative self-talk, it's important to practice talking kindly to yourself.

One way to do this is to imagine yourself as your own best friend. What would you say to a friend who was going through a difficult time? How would you offer support and encouragement? Then, turn these same kind and encouraging words towards yourself.

Another strategy is to use positive affirmations. These are simple statements that you can repeat to yourself, such as "I am worthy and loved" or "I am capable of handling whatever comes my way." By repeating these affirmations regularly, you can shift your mindset towards a more positive and compassionate outlook.

Practicing self-care

Self-care is any activity that helps to improve your physical, emotional, or mental well-being. This can include anything from getting enough sleep to practicing mindfulness meditation to indulging in your favorite hobbies.

The key to practicing self-care is to find activities that nourish and energize you. This might involve trying new things, experimenting with different forms of self-care, or simply doing more of what you already love. Remember, self-care is not a luxury or an indulgence—it's a necessity for our well-being and happiness. By making self-care a priority in your life, you can improve your overall health and happiness.

PRACTICING MAITRI: A GUIDED MEDITATION

Have you ever felt like you're your own worst enemy? Like you're constantly beating yourself up and never giving yourself a break? If so, practicing Maitri meditation might be just what you need. Practicing Maitri meditation involves directing love and kindness towards yourself, which can help to quiet the negative self-talk and self-criticism that so often plague over-thinkers.

Here's a step-by-step guide to practicing Maitri meditation:

1. Find a quiet and comfortable place where you won't be disturbed. Sit in a comfortable position with your back straight and your hands resting on your lap. Close your eyes and take a deep breath in, then exhale slowly. This will help you to relax and clear your mind.

2. Imagine yourself in a peaceful and relaxing place, such as a beach or a forest. Picture yourself surrounded by beauty and tranquility. This visualization can help to calm your mind and create a positive and peaceful state of being.

3. Repeat the following phrases to yourself, focusing on directing love and kindness towards yourself: "May I be happy. May I be healthy. May I be safe. May I live with ease." Repeat these phrases several times, taking deep breaths in between each repetition. Allow yourself to feel the love and kindness flowing towards you and let go of any negative thoughts or self-judgment.

4. As you repeat these phrases, you may also want to visualize yourself in different situations where you could use some self-love and kindness. For example, if you're struggling with a particular challenge, visualize yourself being successful and happy. This can help to reinforce positive feelings and build your sense of self-worth.

5. When you're ready, slowly open your eyes and take a few moments to reorient yourself before getting up. You may feel a sense of calm and peace, or you may feel a surge of positive energy and motivation. Whatever you feel, know that you have taken an important step towards cultivating a sense of self-love and kindness.

Benefits of practicing Maitri meditation

Practicing Maitri meditation can have a range of benefits for your well-being. The practice of directing love and kindness towards yourself can lead to increased self-awareness and self-compassion. It can help you to let go of negative self-talk and self-criticism, and instead focus on your strengths and positive qualities.

Research has shown that self-compassion is linked to lower levels of anxiety, depression, and stress and higher levels of life satisfaction and overall well-being. By practicing Maitri, you are building self-compassion and nurturing your relationship with yourself. This can have a ripple effect on your relationships with others as you learn to treat yourself with kindness and understanding.

The act of practicing Maitri meditation can also be a form of stress relief. When you take a few minutes to sit quietly and focus on positive affirmations, you are giving yourself a break from the hustle and bustle of daily life. This can help to lower your heart rate and blood pressure, as well as reduce feelings of tension and anxiety.

Practicing Maitri meditation can help you to become more present and mindful. By focusing on the present moment and your internal state, you can learn to let go of worries about the past or future. This can lead to increased clarity and focus, and can help you to make more grounded and intentional decisions in your life.

The benefits of practicing Maitri meditation are numerous and impactful. By taking a few minutes each day to direct love and kindness towards yourself, you are nurturing your mental, emotional, and physical well-being. So why not give it a try and see what positive changes it can bring to your life?

Final thoughts

As we come to the end of this chapter, I want to leave you with a few thoughts on the importance of self-love and kindness, and how they can transform your life. Remember, we all have moments of self-doubt and fear, but with the right mindset and tools, we can overcome them. By focusing on ourselves and treating ourselves with the same kindness and understanding that we give to others, we can cultivate a sense of self-worth and confidence that will help us navigate life's challenges.

Practicing Maitri is a powerful tool for cultivating self-love and kindness, and the benefits are many. By taking the time to show ourselves love and compassion, we become better equipped to handle stress, build deeper connections with others, and achieve our goals.

As you go forward, remember to prioritize self-care and self-compassion. Remember that you are worthy of love and kindness and that it is your birthright to experience joy and fulfillment in life.

In the next chapter, we'll delve deeper into the practice of mindfulness and explore how it can help us overcome stress and anxiety, build resilience, and cultivate greater peace and joy in our lives. Get ready to learn new techniques and insights that will help you live a more mindful and present life.

Until then, be kind to yourself, and remember that you are enough.

STEP 10

LIVE MINDFULLY

By now, you have gained a deeper understanding of the reasons behind overthinking, as well as practical strategies to combat it. However, the journey doesn't end here.

Mindfulness is a key component in gaining mastery over your thoughts, feelings, and actions, and can lead to a more fulfilling and purposeful life. In this chapter, we'll explore what mindfulness is, how it can help you overcome overthinking, and practical ways to incorporate mindfulness into your daily life.

By practicing mindfulness, we can gain a deeper awareness and understanding of our thoughts and emotions, and learn to relate to them in a more helpful way. This can lead to a greater sense of control over our thoughts and actions, as well as increased well-being and overall quality of life. So, let's explore what mindfulness is all about.

THE SEVEN PRINCIPLES OF MINDFULNESS

Mindfulness has become a buzzword in recent years, but what exactly is it? At its core, mindfulness is about paying attention to the present moment without judgment. It's a way of cultivating awareness and being fully present in the here and now. In this section, we'll explore the seven principles of mindfulness and why it's important to understand them if you want to have a high quality of life.

1. Non-judging

Non-judging is the first principle of mindfulness, and it's all about learning to be an impartial observer of your own experiences. It means letting go of any preconceived notions or judgments you might have about what is happening in the present moment and simply observing it as it is, without labeling it as "good" or "bad."

This can be a difficult principle to practice, especially if you're used to judging yourself and others. But by practicing non-judging, you can start to cultivate a sense of acceptance and compassion towards yourself and others.

One way to practice non-judging is to simply notice when you're judging yourself or others and try to let go of that judgment without attaching any meaning to it. You can also try to reframe your thoughts in a more neutral or positive way, focusing on the present moment and what you can learn from it.

Research has shown that practicing non-judging can lead to a decrease in stress and anxiety, and an increase in overall well-being and life satisfaction. By learning to observe your experiences without judgment, you can start to cultivate a greater sense of peace and acceptance in your life.

2. Patience

Patience is a key principle of mindfulness. It involves accepting and allowing things to unfold in their own time without getting frustrated or trying to force a particular outcome. Practicing patience can help us to stay calm and centered, even in the midst of challenging situations.

So, what exactly is patience? According to the Greater Good Science Center at UC Berkeley, patience is "the ability to wait for something without getting angry or upset." It's the opposite of impatience, which involves feeling frustrated or annoyed when things don't go our way.

There are many benefits to practicing patience. Research has shown that it can help us to better manage stress, improve our relationships with others, and increase our overall sense of well-being. When we're patient, we're better able to stay present and engaged in the moment, rather than constantly worrying about the future or dwelling on the past.

If you struggle with impatience, don't worry – there are strategies you can use to cultivate more patience in your life. One approach is to practice mindfulness meditation, which can help you to stay present and focused, even when things aren't going your way. Another strategy is to reframe your thinking around patience and see it as an opportunity to practice acceptance of what has come your way.

By practicing patience, you can learn to stay calm and centered, even in the midst of life's challenges. This can help you to better manage stress, improve your relationships with others, and lead a more peaceful and fulfilling life.

3. Beginner's mind

Beginner's mind is a concept in mindfulness that encourages us to approach things with a fresh and open attitude as if we are encountering them for the first time. This helps us to let go of our preconceived notions and judgments and to be more present in the moment.

The benefits of practicing beginner's mind are numerous. By approaching things with a curious and open attitude, we are able to learn and grow more. We are also able to experience things more fully, without the filter of our preconceptions.

So how can we practice beginner's mind? One strategy is to try new things and approach them with a sense of curiosity and wonder. Another strategy is to ask questions about familiar things as if we are seeing them for the first time. We can also cultivate a sense of openness and curiosity in our daily lives by paying attention to our surroundings and noticing the small details we might otherwise overlook.

Overall, practicing beginner's mind can help us to be more present, curious, and engaged in our lives.

4. Trust

Trust is an essential aspect of our lives, and cultivating it is crucial to our overall well-being. When we talk about trust in the context of mindfulness, we refer to developing trust in ourselves and our feelings. Trust is the foundation of any healthy relationship, and it is also the foundation of a healthy relationship with ourselves.

When we trust ourselves, we make better decisions, take more healthy risks, and move forward in life with confidence. We develop a sense of self-reliance that allows us to navigate difficult situations with greater ease. Trusting ourselves also allows us to be more compassionate towards ourselves and others, as we recognize that we are all doing the best we can with the resources we have.

Some strategies for building trust include:

1. **Paying attention to our intuition:** Our intuition is our internal compass, and it is always guiding us toward our highest good. By paying attention to our intuition, we can learn to trust ourselves and our decisions.
2. **Practicing self-compassion:** When we make mistakes or experience setbacks, it is important to treat ourselves with kindness and understanding. Practicing self-compassion allows us to recognize that we are all human and that we are all capable of making mistakes.
3. **Seeking support when needed:** Asking for help when we need it is a sign of strength, not weakness. When we reach out for support, we are demonstrating that we

trust ourselves enough to know when we need assistance.

5. Non-striving

Non-striving encourages us to let go of our desire for a particular outcome or goal. It's about being present in the moment without constantly striving for something more. When we let go of the need to always achieve, we can fully embrace the present moment and experience a sense of freedom and ease.

By practicing non-striving, we can reduce stress and anxiety, increase our sense of well-being, and improve our relationships with others. When we stop pushing and striving, we allow ourselves to be more open and accepting of the world around us.

Here are some strategies for practicing non-striving:

1. **Focus on the process, not the outcome.** When we focus too much on the end result, we can become fixated on success and forget about the importance of the journey. Instead, try to focus on the process and enjoy each step along the way.
2. **Let go of expectations.** When we have expectations about how things should be, we create a sense of pressure and anxiety. By letting go of these expectations, we can experience things as they are and find joy in the present moment.
3. **Embrace uncertainty.** Life is unpredictable, and trying to control everything can lead to stress and anxiety.

Instead, try to embrace uncertainty and see it as an opportunity for growth and learning.

6. Acceptance

Acceptance is a crucial aspect of mindfulness that involves acknowledging and accepting the present moment as it is without trying to change it or judge it. It's important to note that acceptance doesn't mean approval or resignation; rather, it's a way to cultivate a non-judgmental and compassionate attitude towards ourselves and others.

Research has shown that practicing acceptance can have a variety of benefits, including reduced stress and anxiety, improved emotional regulation, and increased life satisfaction. It can also improve our relationships with others by increasing empathy and compassion.

So, how can we practice acceptance in our daily lives? One strategy is to simply acknowledge and observe our thoughts and emotions without judgment, letting them come and go like passing clouds. Another is to practice self-compassion, treating ourselves with the same kindness and understanding that we would offer to a friend.

It's important to note that acceptance doesn't mean giving up on our goals or values; rather, it's a way to approach them with more flexibility and self-compassion. By practicing acceptance, we can cultivate a greater sense of inner peace and resilience, even in the face of difficult situations.

7. *Letting go*

Letting go is a key principle of mindfulness and an important aspect of personal growth. It involves recognizing that we cannot control everything and that we need to release our attachment to things that no longer serve us.

So, what is letting go? Letting go means surrendering our attachment to outcomes and allowing things to unfold naturally. It means releasing the past and accepting the present moment as it is. It means acknowledging that change is a natural part of life and that holding onto things that no longer serve us can hinder our growth.

By releasing our attachment to negative emotions and experiences, we free up mental space and emotional energy for more positive things. We become less stressed and anxious and more present in the moment. We can approach challenges with more clarity and resilience. And we can experience a greater sense of peace and fulfillment in our lives.

So how can we practice letting go? Here are some strategies:

1. **Practice mindfulness meditation** - Mindfulness meditation can help us develop the awareness and acceptance necessary to let go.
2. **Identify what you need to let go of** - Take some time to reflect on the things that are holding you back and write them down.
3. **Make a plan** - Once you've identified what you need to let go of, create a plan for how you will do it. This could

involve seeking support from friends or professionals, practicing self-care, or taking concrete steps to let go of a particular situation or relationship.

4. **Cultivate a growth mindset** - Embrace the idea that failure and setbacks are opportunities for growth and learning. Focus on what you can learn from a difficult experience rather than dwelling on the negative.

By practicing letting go, we can experience greater freedom, peace, and fulfillment in our lives. It can be a challenging process, but with practice and perseverance, we can cultivate the awareness and acceptance necessary to release our attachment to things that no longer serve us.

MINDFULNESS PRACTICES

Mindfulness is a practice that can be cultivated in various ways. Some popular mindfulness practices include meditation, reflection, and bringing focus to the present moment. When we're overthinking, we tend to be either ruminating about the past or worrying about the future. Mindfulness helps us to come back to the present moment and be more aware of our thoughts and feelings.

1. Meditation is a popular mindfulness practice that involves sitting quietly and focusing your attention on your breath, a sound, or a specific word or phrase. This practice can help to calm the mind, reduce stress, and improve overall well-being.

2. Reflection involves introspection and self-awareness. This can include journaling, therapy, or simply taking time to reflect on your experiences and emotions. Reflecting on your thoughts and feelings can help you gain insight into yourself and your patterns of thinking.

3. Bringing focus to the present moment is a simple but effective mindfulness practice that involves redirecting your attention to what is happening right now. This can be as simple as taking a few deep breaths and focusing on the sensations in your body or noticing the sounds and smells around you.

4. Multitasking is a common habit in today's fast-paced world, but it can actually hinder our ability to be present and mindful. When we're multitasking, we're not fully engaged in any one task, and our attention is constantly divided. To be more mindful, try focusing on one task at a time and giving it your full attention.

5. Focusing on the five senses is another mindfulness practice that can help to cultivate awareness and calm. What do you see, smell, hear, taste, or touch right now? You can bring focus to your senses by listening to the sounds in nature, savoring a delicious meal, or simply noticing the feeling of the sun on your skin.

Overall, there are many mindfulness practices that can help us to be more present, calm, and self-aware. By incorporating these practices into our daily lives, we can learn to master our minds and overcome overthinking.

MINDFULNESS EXERCISES

As we've learned in the previous sections, mindfulness can help us gain control over our thoughts, emotions, and lives. But what exactly are mindfulness exercises, and how can they benefit us?

In this section, we'll explore some fun and interactive mindfulness exercises that you can try at home. Whether you're new to mindfulness or have been practicing for a while, these exercises can help you deepen your mindfulness practice and enhance your overall well-being.

Breathing exercise

This exercise involves focusing on your breath as it moves in and out of your body. Find a quiet place to sit comfortably and close your eyes. Take a deep breath in, hold it for a few seconds, and then exhale slowly. Repeat this process for a few minutes, focusing your attention solely on your breath.

Body scan

A body scan involves paying close attention to your physical sensations from head to toe. Lie down on your back and close your eyes. Starting with your toes, focus on each body part and notice any sensations, such as tingling, warmth, or tension. Move slowly up your body, focusing on each part until you reach the crown of your head.

Gratitude journaling

Gratitude journaling involves writing down three things you're grateful for each day. This practice helps you focus on the positive aspects of your life and cultivate a sense of appreciation and contentment.

Mindful walking

This exercise involves walking slowly and mindfully, paying close attention to your surroundings and the sensations in your body. Take a few deep breaths and begin to walk slowly, focusing on each step and the movement of your feet. Notice the sights, sounds, and smells around you, and allow yourself to fully immerse in the present moment.

Loving-kindness meditation

This meditation practice is centered on developing positive emotions like love, kindness, and compassion towards yourself and others. Begin by finding a comfortable, quiet spot where you can sit or lie down. Close your eyes and take a few deep breaths to calm your mind and body.

Next, focus your attention on your heart center, and imagine it filled with warmth and positive energy. As you inhale, silently repeat to yourself, "May I be filled with love and kindness." As you exhale, imagine that you are releasing any negative emotions or tension that you are holding onto.

After a few breaths, imagine extending these feelings of love and kindness to someone you care about, repeating to yourself, "May they be filled with love and kindness." Repeat this phrase a few times, visualizing this person surrounded by love and positivity.

Then, extend these feelings even further by silently repeating the phrase, "May all beings be filled with love and kindness." Imagine extending these feelings of love and compassion to all living beings, both near and far.

Take a few deep breaths and bask in these feelings of love, kindness, and compassion. When you feel ready, slowly open your eyes and bring this positive energy with you as you move through your day.

Final thoughts

You've now learned about the power of mindfulness and how it can help you master your thoughts and improve your life. By understanding the seven principles of mindfulness and practicing different techniques such as meditation and reflection, you can develop a more focused and present state of mind.

Remember, mindfulness takes practice and patience, so don't worry if it doesn't come naturally to you at first. Just keep trying and you'll reap the benefits of a more centered and grounded life.

In the next and final chapter, we'll explore the power of gratitude and how it can transform your life. So, let's continue our journey toward a happier and more fulfilling life.

STEP 11

LIVE GRATEFULLY

D o you ever find yourself so caught up in the problems and challenges of daily life that you forget to appreciate the good things? It's easy to get bogged down by negativity and feel like nothing is going right. However, the truth is that there is always something to be grateful for.

In this chapter, we'll explore the power of gratitude and how it can change your life. Let's dive in and discover how living with gratitude can transform your perspective and bring more joy into your life.

LIVING WITH GRATITUDE

Gratitude is the practice of appreciating and being thankful for what you have in life. Living with gratitude means making this practice a part of our daily lives and allowing it to shape our thoughts, actions, and interactions with the world around us.

Living with gratitude involves developing a mindset that focuses on the positive aspects of our lives rather than dwelling on the negative. It involves being mindful of the good things that we have, recognizing the contributions of others, and feeling thankful for the blessings in our lives.

Research has shown that living with gratitude can have numerous positive effects on our mental, emotional, and physical health. These benefits include:

- Improved mood and overall happiness
- Increased feelings of contentment and satisfaction with life
- Greater resilience in the face of challenges and adversity
- Improved relationships and social connections
- Increased empathy and compassion for others
- Better sleep quality and overall physical health

Living with gratitude is a practice that can be cultivated and developed over time. Some strategies for incorporating gratitude into your daily life include:

- Keeping a gratitude journal to reflect on the good things in your life
- Practicing mindfulness and focusing on the present moment
- Expressing thanks and appreciation to others
- Using positive affirmations and self-talk to reframe negative thoughts

- Engaging in acts of kindness and giving back to others
- Taking time to savor and appreciate enjoyable experiences

By adopting these strategies and making gratitude a part of your daily routine, you can begin to experience the many benefits that come with living with gratitude.

HOW GRATITUDE CAN CHANGE OUR LIVES

Have you ever experienced a moment when you were overwhelmed with a sense of gratitude? Maybe it was a beautiful sunset or a kind gesture from a stranger. In that moment, everything else fades away and you're left with a feeling of warmth and contentment.

Gratitude is a powerful emotion that can transform our lives in ways we never imagined. In this section, we'll explore how living with gratitude can change our lives for the better, and give you practical strategies to cultivate this powerful emotion in your daily life.

Improves self-esteem

When we're feeling down and out, it can be difficult to feel good about ourselves. We may start to criticize ourselves, focusing on our flaws and shortcomings, which can further damage our self-esteem. But what if we shifted our focus to what's going well in our lives? That's where gratitude comes in.

Gratitude allows us to recognize and appreciate the good things in our lives, even the small things. When we practice gratitude regularly, we begin to feel better about ourselves and our worth. We can shift our perspective from self-criticism to self-acceptance, and even self-love.

Research has shown that people who practice gratitude have higher levels of self-esteem than those who don't. They feel more confident in their abilities and are less likely to feel insecure or inadequate. So if you're looking for a way to boost your self-esteem, try focusing on the things you're grateful for and expressing gratitude regularly.

Improves energy and health

Have you ever woken up feeling energized and ready to take on the day? You might have experienced this after a great night's sleep or a morning workout, but did you know that gratitude can also play a role in boosting your energy levels? When we focus on the things we are grateful for, we tend to feel more positive and energized throughout the day.

In addition, studies have shown that gratitude can have a positive impact on our physical health. For example, a study by Emmons and McCullough found that people who kept a gratitude journal for just a few weeks reported fewer physical symptoms and spent more time exercising than those who didn't. Other research has linked gratitude to lower blood pressure, better immune function, and reduced symptoms of depression.

So, not only can gratitude help us feel better mentally, but it can also have a tangible impact on our physical health. It's like a free, natural energy booster and health supplement all in one!

Makes us happier and more optimistic

Have you ever noticed how some people seem to radiate positivity no matter what life throws at them? It's as if they have an inner sunshine that just can't be dimmed. Well, studies show that gratitude may be the key to unlocking that inner sunshine in all of us.

When we practice gratitude, we train our minds to focus on the positive aspects of our lives. By intentionally seeking out and appreciating the good things, we can increase our feelings of happiness and optimism. It's like turning up the brightness on the world around us and seeing everything in a more positive light.

And the best part? The more we practice gratitude, the more our brains become wired to focus on the positive. It's like building a muscle - the more we exercise it, the stronger it becomes. So, not only do we feel happier and more optimistic in the moment, but we also lay the foundation for a more positive outlook in the future.

Makes us more resilient

Life can be unpredictable and full of challenges, but cultivating a grateful mindset can help us build resilience and cope with difficult situations. When we focus on the good things in our lives, we develop a greater sense of perspective and are better able to deal with setbacks and adversity.

In fact, research has shown that gratitude can help us overcome trauma and post-traumatic stress disorder (PTSD). A study conducted by the University of California found that Vietnam War veterans who practiced gratitude showed greater psychological well-being and experienced fewer symptoms of PTSD. By expressing gratitude for the positive aspects of their lives, these veterans were able to develop a more positive outlook and cope with the challenges they faced.

Gratitude can also help us find meaning and purpose in difficult situations. When we face challenges or adversity, it's easy to feel lost or overwhelmed. But by focusing on the good things in our lives, we can find strength and meaning even in tough times. By recognizing and appreciating the good things in our lives, we can build a sense of hope and optimism for the future.

Makes us more generous and forgiving

Have you ever noticed that when someone does something kind for you, you feel a sense of gratitude toward them? That feeling of gratitude can inspire us to do something kind in return or to pay it forward to someone else. Grateful people are more likely to engage in acts of kindness and generosity towards others. This not only benefits the recipients of our generosity, but it also brings us a sense of joy and fulfillment.

Furthermore, gratitude can also help us become more forgiving towards others. When we are grateful for the good things in our lives, we tend to have a more positive outlook and may be more forgiving towards those who have wronged us. We are better able to see things from their perspective and understand that everyone makes mistakes. This doesn't mean that we should condone harmful behavior, but rather that we can choose to let go of anger and resentment and focus on the positive aspects of our lives.

In fact, research has shown that practicing gratitude can increase forgiveness and decrease feelings of revenge. By acknowledging the good in our lives, we may find it easier to forgive those who have hurt us and move forward with a more positive outlook.

Keeps us in the present moment

When we're caught up in the hustle and bustle of our busy lives, it's easy to lose sight of the present moment. Our minds are often preoccupied with our to-do lists, worries, and regrets. However, practicing gratitude can help us stay present and appreciate the beauty in our lives right now.

When we express gratitude for the present moment, we become more aware of our surroundings and the people in our lives. We start to notice the small things that we may have taken for granted before, like the sound of birds chirping outside or the warmth of the sun on our skin. By being present, we can fully engage with our surroundings and the people we love, which can lead to stronger connections and a deeper appreciation for life.

In addition to enhancing our relationships, being present can also have a positive impact on our mental health. When we're fully present in the moment, we're not ruminating on the past or worrying about the future. This can reduce feelings of anxiety and depression and allow us to experience more joy and contentment in our lives.

Lowers stress, anxiety, and negative thoughts

Have you ever noticed how much easier it is to get caught up in negative thoughts and feelings, especially when you're facing difficult situations? It's like a dark cloud hanging over us, clouding our vision and making it hard to see the good things in our lives. That's where gratitude comes in.

When we take the time to appreciate the good things in our lives, no matter how small, it can have a powerful effect on our mental and emotional well-being. Studies have shown that gratitude can lower our levels of stress, anxiety, and negative thoughts, helping us to feel more calm and content.

Think about it – when we're feeling grateful, we're not focused on what's wrong with our lives or what we wish we had. Instead, we're focused on what's going right and what we already have. It's like a mental shift that allows us to see things in a more positive light. This shift can have a domino effect, leading to even more positive changes in our lives.

HOW TO PRACTICE GRATITUDE

Gratitude is a small word with mighty power. It has the ability to change our perspective, improve our mental and physical health, and transform our lives. Yet, it's something we often overlook or take for granted.

In a world that can often feel overwhelming and negative, practicing gratitude can be a lifeline, a beacon of hope and positivity that guides us through the darkness. So, if you're ready to harness the power of gratitude and experience the many benefits it has to offer, keep reading.

In this section, we'll explore simple and effective ways to incorporate gratitude into your daily life.

Start a gratitude journal

Starting a gratitude journal is a great way to start your day on a positive note. By taking the time to reflect on the good things in your life, you can set the tone for the rest of your day. It's a simple and easy practice, but the benefits can be significant.

When you first start your gratitude journal, you might find it hard to come up with things to be grateful for. That's okay! It takes time to cultivate a gratitude mindset. Try thinking of the little things that you might otherwise take for granted, like a warm cup of coffee in the morning, a hug from a loved one, or the sound of birds chirping outside your window. These small moments can have a big impact on our happiness when we take the time to appreciate them. As you continue to practice, you may find that you start to notice more and more things to be grateful for throughout your day.

The beauty of a gratitude journal is that it can be as personal as you want it to be. Some people like to write out detailed descriptions of what they're grateful for, while others prefer to simply jot down a few bullet points. Remember, it's not just about writing them down but really feeling the gratitude in your heart.

One great way to make this a habit is to incorporate it into your routine. Maybe you write down three things you're grateful for each night before bed or during your morning coffee. The key is to find a routine that works for you and stick with it. By making it a regular part of your day, you're training your brain to focus on the good things and building the habit of gratitude.

Express your gratitude to others

Expressing gratitude can be a powerful way to cultivate positive emotions and deepen connections with others. Whether it's a heartfelt thank-you note, a phone call, or simply telling someone in person how much they mean to you, taking the time to express your gratitude can make a big difference.

It's easy to take the people in our lives for granted and assume they already know how much we appreciate them. But expressing gratitude can be a powerful reminder of the impact they have on our lives and can strengthen our relationships with them.

So take a moment to think about the people who have made a positive impact on your life, and find a way to express your gratitude to them. It could be as simple as sending a text message or as elaborate as a lengthy handwritten letter. Whatever form it takes, the act of expressing gratitude is sure to bring a smile to someone's face and lift your own spirits as well.

Use gratitude prompts

Using gratitude prompts is a great way to get started with practicing gratitude. It's common to get stuck when trying to think of things to be grateful for, especially when life gets busy and stressful. That's where prompts can come in handy! They can help spark your creativity and focus your attention on the good things in your life.

One way to use gratitude prompts is to make a list of your favorite prompts and keep them handy in a journal or on your phone. When you're feeling stuck, pull out your list and pick a prompt to reflect on. You might be surprised at how quickly your mind can shift from negative to positive when you focus on the good things around you.

Another way to use prompts is to set aside dedicated time each day to reflect on them. You could do this as part of your daily journaling practice or simply take a few minutes before bed to think about your chosen prompt. The key is to be consistent and intentional with your practice.

Remember, gratitude is a skill that can be cultivated with practice. By incorporating gratitude prompts into your daily routine, you'll be on your way to living a more grateful and fulfilling life.

If you're not sure where to start, here are some gratitude journal prompts to help you get going:

- What is one thing you're grateful for in your life right now?
- What is something good that happened to you today?
- Who is someone in your life that you're thankful for and why?
- What is something about yourself that you appreciate?
- What is a positive change you've made in your life recently that you're proud of?
- What is a material possession you're thankful for and why?
- What is a nature experience that you're grateful for?
- What is something that you take for granted that you're grateful for?
- What is a memory that you're thankful for?
- What is a challenge you've faced that you're now grateful for?

Remember, there's no right or wrong way to journal about gratitude. The key is to make it a regular practice and find joy in the process. Happy journaling!

Final thoughts

Living with gratitude can bring tremendous joy and positivity to our lives. When we take the time to recognize and appreciate the good things in our lives, we shift our focus from what we lack to what we have. This shift in perspective can improve our relationships, our health, and our overall well-being.

By incorporating gratitude practices into our daily lives, we can cultivate a sense of appreciation and thankfulness that will radiate into all aspects of our lives. Whether it's starting a gratitude journal or simply taking a few moments each day to reflect on what we're grateful for, the benefits of living with gratitude are undeniable.

So, let us remember the power of gratitude and the positive impact it can have on ourselves and those around us. Let us embrace the present moment and all the blessings it holds. And let us always remember to be grateful for the opportunity to be alive and experience the beauty of the world around us.

FROM OVERTHINKING TO OVERCOMING: YOU HAVE THE POWER

It's been quite a journey, hasn't it? Throughout this book, we've explored the ins and outs of overthinking and how it affects our lives. We've talked about the different triggers, patterns, and emotions that come along with overthinking, and we've learned how to manage them.

It's no secret that overthinking can be a challenging habit to break, but it's one that's worth tackling. After all, how we think affects how we feel, and how we feel affects how we act. That's why this book is so important - it's all about taking back control of your mind and your life.

But this book isn't just about the individual - it's about all of us. By sharing our stories and our strategies, we can build a community of support and encouragement. We can remind each other that we're not alone, and that there's always hope for change.

Before we dive into the key takeaways from each chapter, I want to remind you of something important: you are not broken. Overthinking is a common and natural tendency. It's not a personal flaw, and it doesn't mean that there's something wrong with you.

The good news is that habits can be changed. You have the power to break the cycle of overthinking and develop healthier thinking patterns. And by picking up this book and reading through the chapters, you've already taken the first step in taking back control of your life and mind.

I also want to let you know that you are not alone. Overthinking is something that many people struggle with, and it's important to recognize that you are not the only one. Billions of people around the world deal with overthinking on a daily basis, so you are definitely not alone in this.

It's okay to ask for help and to seek support when you need it. Remember that there are people who care about you and who want to help you through this. Don't suffer in silence or feel like you have to go through this alone. Reach out to friends, family, or a mental health professional if you need to. There is no shame in asking for help, and it can make a big difference in your journey to overcome overthinking.

Throughout this book, we've explored a variety of ways to combat overthinking and take back control of our lives. Here are some key takeaways from each chapter:

First, we learned that it's important to understand how much thinking is too much and why we overthink in the first place.

By recognizing our tendencies and triggers, we can start to work with them.

Next, we delved into the power of storytelling and how understanding our personal narrative can help us gain insight into our overthinking habits.

We then shifted our focus to the mind itself and learned how to work with our thoughts to promote emotional mastery. We also explored techniques to calm down quickly and get a better night's sleep.

Moving on to decision-making, we discussed how to approach big decisions and tackle indecision. We also looked at ways to overcome feeling overwhelmed and helpless.

We explored the concept of Maitri, or loving-kindness towards oneself, and how it can help us sidestep fear and overthinking. Finally, we discussed the power of gratitude and how it can shift our focus to the positive aspects of our lives. By putting these steps into practice, you can start to break free from the cycle of overthinking and live a more fulfilled and present life.

Overcoming overthinking is not an easy feat, but it is possible. Take Kim, for example. Kim struggled with overthinking for years and it was affecting every aspect of her life. She would obsess over decisions, replay conversations in her head, and worry about the future. It was exhausting, and she felt like there was no way out.

But Kim didn't give up. She started by understanding her triggers and patterns and then worked on mastering her emotions. She practiced mindfulness and self-compassion, and slowly but surely, she began to see changes in her thought patterns. Kim learned to take control of her thoughts rather than allowing them to control her.

Today, Kim is a different person. She is more confident and at peace with herself, and she is able to enjoy life in a way she never thought possible. So if you're struggling with overthinking, know that you, too, can overcome it.

Now that you have learned about the different ways to combat overthinking, it's time to put them into practice. Remember, change doesn't happen overnight, so be patient with yourself and celebrate small victories along the way.

If you found this book helpful, **please leave a review on Amazon**. Your review can help others who are struggling with overthinking find the support they need.

Scan the QR code below for a quick review!

Don't let your worries control your life. Instead, focus on what you can control, and take action to create the life you want.

You have within you the strength, resilience, and resources to overcome overthinking and live a more present, fulfilled life. It won't be easy, but it will be worth it. Embrace the process, celebrate small victories along the way, and know that you are capable of creating positive change in your life.

So take a deep breath, hold your head up high, and step confidently into the future.

You got this!

REFERENCES

Acupressure for Stress and Anxiety. (n.d.). Memorial Sloan Kettering Cancer Center. https://www.mskcc.org/cancer-care/patient-education/acupressure-stress-and-anxiety#

American Psychological Association. "The Psychology of Emotions." APA, 2020.

Antonioli, C., Reveley, M. A., & Monnazzi, P. (2005). The Effect of Physical Exercise on Plasma Beta-Endorphin and Anxiety in Patients with Chronic Obstructive Pulmonary Disease. Respiratory Medicine, 99(12), 1559-1564. https://doi:10.1016/j.rmed.2005.03.004

Beck, J. S. (2011). Cognitive behavior therapy: Basics and beyond. Guilford Press.

Davidson, R. J., & Begley, S. (2012). The emotional life of your brain. Penguin.

Davis, D. M., & Hayes, J. A. (2011). What Are the Benefits of Mindfulness? A Practice Review of Psychotherapy-Related Research. Psychotherapy, 48(2), 198–208. https://doi.org/10.1037/a0022062

Getting into Water Can Help with Anxiety. (2015, October 5). PubMed Central (PMC). https://www.ncbi.nlm.nih.gov/pmc/articles/PMC4657308/

Harvard Health Publishing. (2021, March 23). Benefits of mindfulness. Harvard Health. https://www.helpguide.org/harvard/benefits-of-mindfulness.htm

Hölzel, B. K., Carmody, J., Evans, K. C., Hoge, E. A., Dusek, J. A., Morgan, L., ... & Lazar, S. W. (2010). Stress reduction correlates with structural changes in the amygdala. Social cognitive and affective neuroscience, 5(1), 11-17.

Jha, A. P., Krompinger, J., & Baime, M. J. (2007). Mindfulness training modifies subsystems of attention. Cognitive, Affective, & Behavioral Neuroscience, 7(2), 109-119.

Kryger, M. H., Roth, T., & Dement, W. C. (2017). Principles and practice of sleep medicine. Elsevier.

Mayo Clinic. (2021). Anxiety disorders. https://www.mayoclinic.org/diseases-conditions/anxiety/symptoms-causes/syc-20350961

National Institute of Mental Health. (2020). Post-Traumatic Stress Disorder.

https://www.nimh.nih.gov/health/topics/post-traumatic-stress-disorder-ptsd/index.shtml

Padesky, C. A. (1994). Schema change processes in cognitive therapy. Clinical Psychology & Psychotherapy, 1(5), 267-278.

Pedersen, Anette Fischer et al. "Risk factors for stress reactions - a longitudinal study of police officers during work re-organization." BMC medicine vol. 18,1 75. 7 Apr. 2020, https://doi:10.1186/s12916-020-01668-w

Sansone, R. A., & Sansone, L. A. (2010). Gratitude and well being: The benefits of appreciation. Psychiatry (Edgmont), 7(11), 18–22.

The Science of Belly Breathing. (n.d.). Medical News Today. https://www.medicalnewstoday.com/articles/diaphragmatic-breathing

Westressfree. (n.d.). The negative effects of overthinking – What does it do to our health? https://westressfree.com/the-negative-effects-of-overthinking-what-does-it-do-to-our-health/

Wignall, N. (2019). 7 Psychological reasons you overthink everything. Nick Wignall. https://nickwignall.com/overthinking/

Wood, A. M., Froh, J. J., & Geraghty, A. W. (2010). Gratitude and well-being: A review and theoretical integration. Clinical Psychology Review, 30(7), 890-905. https://doi.org/10.1016/j.cpr.2010.03.005

Wood, A. M., Joseph, S., & Maltby, J. (2009). Gratitude predicts psychological well-being above the big five facets. Personality and Individual Differences, 46(4), 443-447. https://doi.org/10.1016/j.paid.2008.11.012

www.ingramcontent.com/pod-product-compliance
Lightning Source LLC
Chambersburg PA
CBHW070717130626
46553CB00005B/2030